THE
LOVE
WORKBOOK

A GUIDE TO HAPPINESS
IN YOUR
PERSONAL RELATIONSHIPS

THE
LOVE WORKBOOK

A GUIDE TO HAPPINESS
IN YOUR PERSONAL RELATIONSHIPS

David R. Lima, M.S.W.

SUPER 6 PUBLISHING

THE LOVE WORKBOOK
First Printing 1988, Revised Edition 1999
Copyright 1988, 1999 by David R. Lima
Printed in the United States of America

ISBN 1-893733-00-9 Paperback

SUPER SIX PUBLISHING
8353 MENTOR AVE.
MENTOR, OHIO 44060
A Division of David R. Lima, ACSW, Inc.
www.lima-associates.com
(800) 810-9011

Acknowledgment is made to Warner Bros. Music for permission
to reprint portions of lyrics from
"What is This Thing Called Love?" by Cole Porter.
Copyright 1929 WARNER BROS., INC. (Renewed)
All Rights Reserved
Used By Permission

Although The Love Workbook provides accurate and authoritative information concerning the topics covered, it does not take the place of a competent professional in the event counseling or other professional services are required. This book does not constitute, and should not be construed as, the practice of any regulated professional service.

To Nancy, my wife, and Christopher, Julie, and Stefanie, our children.

We've worked at it.

CONTENTS

XI   FOREWORD

XIII   INTRODUCTION

17   CHAPTER 1 .... What Is This Thing Called Love?

29   CHAPTER 2 .... What Do You Want To Get Out Of This Relationship?

39   CHAPTER 3 .... Keeping Your Emotions Under Control

51   CHAPTER 4 .... Negotiation: The Art of Compromise and Change

65   CHAPTER 5 .... Listing Your Specific Expectations and Defining Exactly What You Mean

79   CHAPTER 6 .... The Importance of Your Expectations, Scoring Your Partner's Performance and Setting Priorities

91   CHAPTER 7 .... Negotiating and Coming To Terms

109   CHAPTER 8 .... Continuing The Process: Review Of Previously Selected Expectations, Recontracting and Selection of Additional Expectations

121   APPENDIX A .... What If Something Goes Wrong! Troubleshooting The Process - Part I

147   APPENDIX B .... What If Something Goes Wrong! Troubleshooting The Process - Part II

157   APPENDIX C .... Additional Methods and Techniques

163   APPENDIX D .... Negotiating Process Form and List of Desirable Traits

171   APPENDIX E .... Additional Selected Lists of Expectations

181   APPENDIX F .... Suggested Reading List

185   APPENDIX G........ Sources of Professional Help

187   REFERENCES

189   INDEX

191   ABOUT THE AUTHOR

FOREWORD

THE LOVE WORKBOOK is exactly what its name implies—a book that concretely shows you, the reader, how to actively work at improving your love, marital, and sex relationships. It also closely follows two main principles of rational emotive behavior therapy (REBT):

First, whenever you engage in self-defeating feelings and behaviors, look closely at what you are doing—and, especially, at what you are telling yourself—to create your needless self-sabotaging. Zero in on your absolutist commands—your dogmatic shoulds, oughts, and musts—by which you keep upsetting yourself, actively dispute them, and rationally rip them up until you rarely any longer believe them.

Second, as you keep surrendering your demands that unfortunate things that happen to you must not exist and that you can't stand it when they do, work hard at changing these things and at improving the poor environment in which you live. How? By problem-solving, by skill training, and by collaborating with others in your social, business, and affectional life.

REBT, then, consists of changing your self-sabotaging thoughts, feelings, and actions and of actualizing yourself and increasing your enjoyments. It is famous for its advocacy of the former; but it also importantly includes the latter. THE LOVE WORKBOOK nicely teaches both these basic elements of REBT.

Specifically, it clearly and incisively shows you how to interrupt and eliminate your affectional blockings—especially your feelings of anxiety, depression, rage, and self-pity. But going far beyond this, it describes many practical, workable methods of fostering communication, recharging your love and sex life, increasing your assertiveness, and using other valuable techniques of affectional rapprochement and enduring attachment.

Just as REBT is always cognitive and behavioral, so is this book. It shows you how to think differently and thereby unupset yourself about virtually any of the usual hassles of mating and relating. But it also gives you many solid work exercises that demonstrate how to <u>act</u> less disturbed, more lovingly, and more enjoyably. As its title says, this love book is also a work book. David Lima has beautifully combined some of the most useful methods of thought and action to produce a practical and valuable guide to love and life. Read them and use them—to change yourself and the conditions that may now interfere with your relationship goals.

Albert Ellis, Ph.D.
Albert Ellis Institute for Rational Emotive Behavior Therapy
Formerly the Institute for Rational-Emotive Therapy
45 East 65th Street
New York, NY 10021

INTRODUCTION

This is a practical book about acquiring one of life's most sought after and important commodities, love. This book will help you understand what love is and how to work to get it. However, what this book will not do is portray love as easy to get if only you "open yourself to it". That's what makes this book surprisingly and refreshingly different. The Love Workbook presents in a straight-forward, clear and precise manner methods for achieving love and happiness in your relationships with others.

The Search for Love and Happiness

We spend a great deal of time and energy searching for love and happiness. Periodically we are consumed with the task of finding that "special someone" to fulfill our love needs. The search seems to permeate every aspect of our being.

After finding someone and "falling in love", our vulnerability and capacity for error rise dramatically. If we begin to experience intense feelings of irritation, anger, anxiety or depression and these negative emotions combine with feelings of helplessness and hopelessness, the newly found partners may very well distance themselves from each other. A new idea begins to emerge - "I think I'm falling out of love".

Love Defined

Love is difficult to describe because of the many, and often times confusing, ideas we have about it. However, I believe love is not much different from other human emotions and, contrary to the opinion that it defies definition, I believe love is rather easily defined.

Love is that strong positive feeling that attracts one person to another. We experience this feeling when our expectations, whatever they might be, are being met.

We "feel" attracted toward another person when they, through hard work, meet our expectations. We want them around. We may even crave their presence. *From the awareness of our own craving* we happily conclude "I think I'm falling in love".

When our partner does what we want, we feel happy and love what they are doing. And, we begin to love the person who is doing it.

A Guide To Happiness in Your Personal Relationships

I decided to call this publication THE LOVE WORKBOOK because I believe that love is more likely to occur when it is earned, that work is required to get it and work will be required to keep it. Although I can't guarantee that the work involved in using this guide will actually bring you love, I feel certain that it will at least prepare you for the love experience.

The work you do in this guide may lead to further work with a marriage counselor or a professional therapist, or it may be used by your therapist in conjunction with the counseling you are already receiving. The work you do in this guide may lead to decisions concerning your current relationship. If you have not achieved the love and happiness you want in spite of all your efforts, including the help of a counselor or this guide, you may decide to leave the relationship.

However, after people leave a relationship it isn't very long until most find themselves in another one. We appear to be a rather gregarious lot and this pairing process comes as no surprise. Most of us look for happiness within the context of a human relationship. That means once again we are faced with the task of asking for and getting our expectations met, of finding out what our partner wants and trying to meet our partner's expectations. Clearly, we are faced with the ongoing task of WORKING at our relationships - **managing the process between two individuals.** Managing a relationship doesn't sound romantic, and, for the most part, it isn't. But, I believe if we are going to lead happier lives, then we better learn to manage our relationships. And that's what I hope this workbook can do for you - teach you how to manage your personal relationships in a more effective, more loving way.

One of the most significant barriers to your continued use and completion of the tasks in this book is called LFT. LFT means 'low frustration tolerance' and keeps people from expending the necessary effort for completing tasks and reaching goals. LFT causes us to procrastinate. If you are a 'procrastinator' and are likely to experience difficulty in completing these assignments, please turn immediately to Appendix A and read the first section on LFT. Go ahead, do it now!!!

I mentioned in the second paragraph that strong negative emotions often get in the way of people overcoming their relationship difficulties. A therapy originated by Albert Ellis some forty years ago has proven very effective in helping individuals overcome emotional disturbances that so often lead to misery and ineffective problem-solving. Dr. Ellis, one of the most prominent psychologists of our time, calls this therapy REBT, Rational

Emotive Behavior Therapy. REBT, when practiced by someone who has learned to use it, enables control of excessive negative emotions like anger, depression, and anxiety. As I point out later in this guide, this is especially important in relationships where significant differences exist. Differences often lead to excessive negative emotions. This can be problematic for two people trying to solve their differences. **Straight thinkers with clear heads are more effective relationship managers.**

This workbook is designed to help you achieve more happiness in your personal relationships with others. Even if you are already producing happiness, it may not be at levels you desire. Therefore, additional work may be required to achieve those levels. Remember, *you don't have to be sick to get better.*

This book will be used primarily by married couples, but it is designed for use by other paired relationships as well - parent/child, friend/friend, non-married pairs, co-workers, those who are about to get married, or any other paired relationship where more happiness is desired. So, let's get down to work!

Chapter 1

———⟶✦⟵———

WHAT IS THIS THING CALLED LOVE?

NOTES

Chapter 1

WHAT IS THIS THING CALLED LOVE?

What is this thing called love?
This funny thing called love?
Just who can solve its mystery?
Why should it make a fool of me?
I saw you there one wonderful day.
You took my heart and threw it away.
That's why I ask the Lawd in Heaven above,
What is this thing called love?

The refrain from this 1920's song brings to mind the mystery long associated with love. The lyrics ask what love is, but give no answers. The implication is that love is not able to be understood. Love can only be felt. And, above all, when you think you've got it, that loving feeling that is, don't let go of it. After all, you may never get another chance. And don't bother to think about it. True love does not require thinking.

That's exactly what millions of people all over the world do, day in and day out. They fall in love with another person and, based on the presence of these feelings, decide to form a relationship. Then they find themselves facing a myriad of problems and issues not thought possible. The individuals involved didn't think very much, they mostly felt.

"But isn't that what you're supposed to do?", you might ask. "Go with your feelings, that is? Are not my feelings 'beacons in the night' showing me the way?"

These are legitimate questions based on what is commonly taught in our culture. We are taught to <u>reason using our emotions</u>. "Emotional reasoning" is thinking that a feeling, and its presence in your gut, <u>is proof of something that is right and true</u>, and any action that follows must be right and true. So, most people 'follow their hearts'. In my opinion, this is very risky business. Could you imagine a manager of a business or corporation making decisions on the basis of feelings of the heart rather than information and facts? Partners who decide to form a relationship primarily on the basis of intense emotions often find themselves scratching their heads in disbelief when problems push to the surface. When this happens partners tend to get very discouraged. Then, feeling desperate and frustrated, they start blaming each other or themselves.

Most relationships are not able to withstand blaming without eroding trust, cooperativeness and love. Relationships are bound to deteriorate when this happens. I believe our high divorce rate is testimony to this phenomena and to the unpreparedness of so many for the rigors of a marital relationship. When it becomes too much for the couple to handle the deteriorating situation themselves, that's when I see them for counseling. Rarely do I see couples *before* they make the decision to pair up. Given the way we view love, why would anyone come to me about what they already know "in their hearts" to be "right and true"?

"To be loved or not to be loved, that is the question," and for some, the only question that matters.

Because 'love' feelings are so strong, some people seem to be *overly determined* and even *desperately driven* to experience 'love', regardless of other considerations. Such excessive determination may be an indication of serious problems quite removed from the legitimate or rational search for love.

In some instances the feeling of anxiety may promote desperate behavior and the decision to form a relationship. Here's the way it works:

- ◆ First, you tell yourself you <u>need</u> to be in a relationship with a certain person.
- ◆ Second, you tell yourself you <u>need</u> their love.
- ◆ Third, after declaring that you <u>need</u> it, it becomes <u>absolutely necessary</u> that you have it. (You see, a <u>need</u> is an absolute necessity, no ifs, ands, or buts about it.)
- ◆ Fourth, you begin to experience <u>anxiety</u> and <u>fear</u> that you might not get it, or, if you have it, that you might lose it.

When we identify one thing as a "need", we eliminate <u>all other alternatives</u> or possibilities for satisfying ourselves. We <u>box ourselves</u> in. Imagine being "all boxed in" and <u>not</u> having what you "need"! Imagine the feeling of anxiety and fear that you would experience! Here's what people typically say when they are desperately in love - "Without you, life isn't worth living!" or, "I can't go on without you!" or, "You make me a whole person!" or, "Without you, I am nothing!" Desperate expressions of love are filled with the idea of need and self-downing (unless the love of their life is present). Many people are VERY serious when they think of love as a requirement, and think less of themselves if they fail to have the love they need. Self downing and feelings of worthlessness may be so extreme that the person thinks about or actually commits suicide.

MORE ON NEEDFUL THINKING AND COGNITIVE MUTATIONS

The idea of needing something originates from a sound and reasonable way of thinking, namely, "I want something or someone very much". Who could fault anyone for simply wanting and speaking of that want? However, when this reasonable idea is transformed into an unreasonable idea, problems usually begin. The act of changing an idea is called "cognitive transmutation". Look at the example below:

Original Idea: "I *want* a chocolate ice cream cone very much."
[*Cognitive mutation occurs*.]
New Idea: "I *must* have a chocolate ice cream cone now!"

This newly formed idea, which I call a cognitive mutation, now resides in your mind and becomes part of your automatic thinking. **You may not be aware of the subtle change that has occurred and view the new idea as accurate, factual and truthful.** You may begin to use this new idea when making decisions about your behavior. For example, when you have a 'taste' for ice cream the next day, and you think "I must have a chocolate ice cream cone" and you can't or don't have one, you are likely to generate very specific emotions. These emotions tend to be excessive and negative. Imagine the frustration you would experience when you can't or don't get a chocolate ice cream cone and you are thinking "I must have a chocolate ice cream cone, now!" Anger and irritation most assuredly will follow. This is all quite unnecessary and avoidable and the solution is remarkably quite simple. Change the new idea back to its original form, namely "I want a chocolate ice cream cone very much, but that doesn't mean I must have it!" Put the transmutation process in reverse, flush the mutated idea out of your mind replacing it with your beginning preference!

Reasonable thought:
"I want (desire) something very much."

Emotional Consequence:
Determination to get it.

[Irrational Mental Jump-Shift or Cognitive Mutation]

Mutated Idea:
"I must have what I want!"

New Emotional Consequence:
Desperation to get it and a lot of frustration, anger and hostility if it is not gotten
OR until it is gotten.

[Cognitive Mutation Reversed, Flushing and Replacement]

Corrected View:
"Yes, I want it very much, but that doesn't mean I must have it."

Corrected Emotional Consequence:
Determination to get it.

Exercise: Needful Thinking

Close your eyes. Think of something you really believe you need. Get it vividly in your mind's eye. Take a minute to focus upon it. See yourself with it. Focus on your feelings. Now, imagine yourself without it. Take a minute to see yourself without it. Open your eyes.

How did you feel when you "saw" yourself with it? How did your feelings change when you "saw" yourself without it? Write these reactions down and share them with your partner.

THE NEED FOR LOVE

When I see individuals or couples in my office, I usually try to find out whether the "I must have love" mutated idea is present in their thinking. Unfortunately, in almost every instance it is! In addition, the belief that everyone else "needs" love is there as well. Clients are surprised when I suggest the idea might not be true, and that their feelings of depression, anger, and anxiety may be related to this idea.

Clients frequently argue this point and some have used data from "infants failure to thrive" research as evidence for the need for love. Briefly, the data show that "retarded" growth and development occurs when infants are not cared for lovingly. And, in fact, this is true. However, people erroneously conclude that it is the missing love that causes the failure to thrive. In fact, it has been shown that missing loving **BEHAVIOR** is causative. Loving behavior includes a lot of physical stimulation, touching, stroking, cooing, smiling, etc., stimulating the central nervous system. This stimulation creates a more complex nervous system capable of dealing with the increasingly complex demands of life. So, if infants are stimulated early in life they will usually thrive, whether or not that stimulation is *love motivated*. However, I do believe caring behavior is a lot more likely to occur if the caretaker or parent is motivated by love.

People "need love" and/or "to be loved" for many different reasons. Albert Ellis, in a paper entitled Unhealthy Love: Its Causes and Treatment, lists the fear of uncertainty and the fear of not being able to take care of oneself as primary causes for "unhealthy" love. Paul Hauck, in his book Marriage is a Loving Business, lists many unhealthy reasons for tying the knot. For each of those listed, I have added the *"needful"* thinking component.

a. To spite your parents. *(I need to win, need to be in charge, need to have control over my parents. I'll show them, I'll get married!)*

b. To overcome inferiority feelings. *(I need to feel better about myself, need to have approval from others in order not to be or feel like a louse. I'll overcome those feelings when I get married!)*

c. To be a therapist for your mate. *(I need to see myself as better than the poor soul I've married. Because my partner has so many problems, he/she needs the help that I'll be able to give.)*

d. Fear of spinsterhood or bachelorhood. *(I need to be with someone, I need to avoid being alone. If I am alone it will prove my lack of worth.)*

e. Fear of independence. *(I need to have someone take care of me because I can't do it for myself. If I try, I am sure to fail.)*

f. On the rebound. *(I need to know I'm desirable to others, I need to prove to myself and my past partner that I'm not undesirable.)*

g. Fear of hurting other people. *(I need to be nice to other people because I must avoid their disapproval of me. I need their approval.)*

h. Because you were in love or had sex. *(I need to follow my love feelings no matter what because my love feelings are beacons of truth to be followed without question. Sex and love are the same, and since I've had sex, I must have a loving relationship with the person with whom I've been intimate.)*

i. To escape an unhappy home. *(I need to get away because I can't stand the rotten situation I'm in.)*

OTHER MASKS OF LOVE

Biologic, romantic, and sociologic explanations of the pairing phenomena exist and account, along with the unhealthy explanations noted above, for the sometimes desperate and preoccupative love behavior of humans. Although there is nothing innately wrong with love stemming from any of these areas, I believe they lack the power to sustain the relationship over time.

Biologic

There is no denial of the role biology plays in the pairing phenomena. Sexual hormones and equipment are readied for use early in life and explored by all. If one's sexuality is explored alone, there seems to be a universal longing to experience it with another person.

Being biologically motivated has, at best, a limited benefit for a number of reasons. First, we tend to get bored with most things that are one-dimensional. Change and variety appear to be highly prized and sought after by most individuals. New and different goals are sought and explored by many of us. Second, we age and so does our biological structure. We may become less physically attractive with aging, at least according to society's generally accepted view of beauty (young, under the age of 22, taut skin, good muscle tone, etc.). None of us remain as "beautiful" or as "handsome" as we once were. Third, biological reproduction necessitating the physical union of two people becomes less important as time goes on and age increases. The desire for offspring diminishes in time. This is especially true if a couple already has a number of children.

Romantic

Romantic notions often are motivating forces in the formation of intimate relationships. Basically, romantic notions are soft on reality and have a high degree of fantasy imbedded in them. Some romantic notions are downright false and have no basis in fact.

Some of the most frequently held romantic notions go something like this:
> "Love is the only thing that matters."
> "Love is the only important sustaining force in the universe."
> "The absence of love at any time in your life makes life meaningless."
> "I must have love to live."
> "My partner must show me love all the time or it means my partner doesn't truly love me."

A person who acts on the basis of any of the above ideas may be perceived by others as being "madly in love". Individuals in this situation can be whisked away by their emotions and passions only to face serious problems later when the romantic bloom fades and fails to materialize.

Sociologic

Social rules and standards prescribe love behaviors as well. These rules provide a significant amount of added pressure to form a "love" partnership.

> "You've been going with her/him for so long, when are you getting married?"
> "You two are so right for each other!"
> "You're not getting any younger you know!"
> "You're not going to find anyone out there any better, at least for you!"
> "Sensible people settle down and get married."

Much like the biologic and romantic influences described above, sociologic reasons for pairing are unlikely to have the fuel to power the relationship over the long run. "Social love", "biological love" and "romantic love" can easily be mistaken for "true love".

Exercise: Reasons for a Relationship

Sit down with paper and pencil. Make an inventory of the reasons you have paired or are wanting to pair with another person. Do you find any of the above reasons on your list? Do the same thing, make an inventory of reasons for pairing, for other people you know, your friend, co-worker, mother, father, sister, brother, or your prospective partner. Keep these lists for future reference and discussion.

HEALTHY LOVE

So, what is true love exactly? Paul Hauck, in his book, Marriage is a Loving Business, defines it clearly. Love is that positive emotion you feel toward another person when that person is meeting your expectations. It's that simple, but let me explain further. Loving and liking what a person is doing for you (because you want them to) and wanting to be with the person who is doing it, seems to be a natural reaction for most people. We like to be around people who treat us well, and we avoid those who do not. Liking or disliking a person, based on how they are treating us, follows in rather automatic fashion. If the situation continues, and intensifies, we may begin to say that we "love" the person who is doing the behavior, or "hate" the person who is not doing what we want.

Love grows and develops in three steps:
1. Someone has and gives us something that we value;
2. We like their behavior;
3. We like them for acting that way.

Love is a very selfish emotion. This idea may be difficult for people to understand and accept since love is viewed by most of us as an unselfish emotion. In our culture love is characterized as giving and never-ending. However, marriage counseling data indicate that people "fall out of love" frequently, and seem to because their expectations are not being met. People who "fall in love" do so because their expectations are being met or they anticipate them being met. *Love is "me-oriented".*

Some might question whether this view of love is moral. Albert Ellis and Irving Becker, in their book <u>A Guide to Personal Happiness</u> provide moral justification for the pursuit of individual happiness:

a. Other people are not going to do it for you, or are not likely to give you happiness even if you give it to them first;

b. If you don't go for your own happiness, others may think you foolish or take advantage of you;

c. If you don't find your own happiness, you may hate yourself for sacrificing it for other less enjoyable goals;

d. Planning your life and its direction resulting in happiness may be an enjoyable pursuit in and of itself;

e. Striving for happiness makes you more valuable to others, and consequently, more lovable - therefore, your opportunities for loving relationships increase; and,

f. Striving for happiness leads to a more honest relationship with others because you're more honest with your personal agenda.

Pursuing happiness as you define it makes sense. Being honest with others in that pursuit rather than hiding it will give you better chances of getting happiness. And, when you get happiness, you might even find "love" there also, if you're lucky enough to find a partner who meets your expectations. **Working it out so that each of you can <u>achieve happiness together</u> is the goal of this book.**

I firmly believe this is possible, but it does require hard work and effort. If you are the kind of reader that skips things like the 'Introduction', please go back and read it. There is something there that is very important for you to know and may have a significant impact on completing many of the exercises presented in this book. If you have already read the 'Introduction', read on!

NOTES

Chapter 2

———⟫●⟪———

WHAT DO YOU WANT TO GET OUT OF THIS RELATIONSHIP?

NOTES

Chapter 2

WHAT DO YOU WANT TO GET OUT OF THIS RELATIONSHIP?

Defining goals, objectives, and purposes for living is a difficult task. People spend relatively little time thinking about such matters. When they do, they often get bogged down and are eager to give it up. More than likely they go through life following a prescribed plan, set for them by parents, others, and their culture. When I ask clients what they want from a relationship, they are puzzled by the question and find it difficult to respond. If there is a response, it's usually vague. Or the response is simply, "I don't know!" This is not a surprise, given the lack of clarity most people have about their goals in life. When I suggest the overall purpose might be **to get as much happiness out of life for as long as possible**—the response is, "Oh sure, of course, what else!" Conclusion: People take happiness for granted, expect to have it, but spend little time consciously thinking and planning about <u>how</u> to get it.

The Case of Vern and Sue

Sue had been feeling dissatisfied with her marriage to Vern for about two years when she called for an appointment. He wasn't interested in counseling, but had agreed to it reluctantly. They both sat before me with Sue doing most of the talking. She described their increasing conflicts and arguments, lessening communication and sexual contacts. He sat quietly. She continued to identify additional problems and went on to describe what she wanted from Vern. He sat quietly. Obviously, Sue had been doing a lot of thinking about her relationship with Vern.

After about 15 minutes I turned and looked at Vern and asked him what he thought the problems were in their relationship. He responded, "I thought everything was fine!" He went on to indicate his surprise that she felt the way she did. He also said that he felt it unnecessary that they have counseling. I asked what he wanted from Sue. At first he said he didn't know, that he hadn't thought about it. Then, after about

30 seconds of silence, he said he just wanted to be married. Vern's responses indicate little or no thinking about what he wanted out of his relationship with Sue. He "just wanted to be married!".

Roads to happiness are many and varied, especially when you add another person to the mix. Since each individual has his/her own set of ideas, may only be vaguely aware of them, hasn't spent much time planning for happiness, we often find "the blind leading the blind". When the "blind" pursuit of happiness occurs, it frequently results in just the opposite - unhappiness.

It seems this lack of interest in or concern for the "how" of finding happiness follows from some common romantic notions taught in our culture and discussed in Chapter 1. Romantic thoughts block the systematic exploration of expectations you might have of a partner. "It just isn't right, and (if you have to talk about it and plan for it) it doesn't reflect true love". **True love should allow you to achieve happiness effortlessly**.

Of course, there may be other reasons for not sharing your expectations with your partner. You may fear that your partner will not agree or approve, or that you will not get your way, or you will be indebted to your partner if you do get your way. These and other reasons lead many to be reluctant to explore their hopes, desires and wants, sacrificing intimacy and happiness in the process.

The Case of Fran and Mel

Mel had recently become concerned about his marriage to Fran because of her growing disinterest in sex. She seemed to avoid contact with him as much as she could. She frequently refused him outright, and when they did have sex, she complained she didn't enjoy it. In fact, she stopped actively participating and required Mel to do "all the work". Not only was this frustrating to Mel, but he had begun to worry that there was something seriously wrong. After thorough explorations with both individuals in separate sessions, I was convinced that there was little wrong in their relationship except the sex.

That's when I suggested an "Intimacy Program" as a way to improve their sexual relationship. I explained the intimacy program to them as a series of sensual and

33

CHAPTER 2 / What Do You Want to Get Out of This Relationship?

sexual exercises that would be assigned to them to do in the privacy of their home. I further explained that the program was designed to get the couple to do physically pleasurable things to and with each other. In addition, it would give them a chance to relate to each other on a social and emotional level for a minimum of 4 hours a week. Fran was appalled. She couldn't see how such a thing would help and was quite convinced that she wouldn't be able to participate. When pressed further she revealed a very strong belief that when it came to lovemaking, it should be spontaneous and natural. In fact, she believed that if you had to plan it and "just acted" like you liked it, it was tantamount to admitting to your partner that you really didn't love him. In other words, love, if present, should create the sexual satisfaction in their relationship, not talking, planning, or exercises. In Fran's mind, planning something like this was dead wrong.

I have the opposite belief. I believe you have many ideas about your happiness and an obligation to share these desires and expectations with your partner. How else will you or your partner know if your expectations are, can or should be met? This sharing should occur before any sizable relationship investment is made by either partner. By carrying out the tasks and assignments in this book you will learn how to calculate, with a higher degree of confidence, the satisfaction and happiness capabilities of a relationship.

Ellis and Becker in <u>A Guide to Personal Happiness</u> put it quite succinctly. Your right to determine for yourself what you want (in order to be happy) and to pursue your goals for happiness are based on two important ideas:

(1) Putting yourself and your happiness first; and,
(2) In the pursuit of your happiness, not unnecessarily harming others.

I believe these rules prescribe a moral and ethical way for finding happiness. We live on a planet with six billion people each busily pursuing happiness. Only you and you alone can or will take responsibility for your personal happiness. So, when you do it (take charge of your personal happiness), remember six billion other people are doing it also. Try hard not to interfere with another person's pursuit of happiness. Why? Because they just might interfere with yours. **This <u>dual</u> concern for yourself <u>and</u> for others is an important key to finding happiness.**

EXPECTATIONS

It is strongly suggested that expectations be *rational and practical*. Rational expectations help you achieve your goal of *happiness* and have *reality* (data) to back them up. It is fairly easy to determine whether you are happy or unhappy. Simply ask yourself whether you feel happy or unhappy. You are able to do this because your feelings are immediately accessible to you. You know how you feel! It is not as easy to determine whether your expectations are supported by reality (and therefore, achievable). This requires that you search for data to "back up" your expectations.

THE SEARCH FOR DATA

How do you go about looking for evidence to support your ideas? Let's say you expect your partner to give you affection. Ask two questions:

"Is it realistic to expect my partner to act affectionately toward me?"

"Will I be happy if my partner treats me with affection?"

1. Because you want to feel good, and getting affection makes you feel good, it meets the criteria of getting you happiness.
2. If your partner is capable and willing to give you affection, it makes sense to take advantage of it.
3. Since affection within a relationship is sanctioned by society, it allows you to have ready access to something you want. Access it!
4. When people treat each other with affection, they tend to get along better. This makes life easier.
5. Affection fosters cooperativeness and a greater likelihood that affection will be reciprocated.

When you find supportive data like those listed above, add the expectation to your list.

Exercise: Rational and Practical Expectations

On a sheet of paper, list as many additional reasons that support the expectation for an affectionate partner.

35

CHAPTER 2 / What Do You Want to Get Out of This Relationship?

Condemnation
I'm worthless
Awfuliz.
I can't stand
Always / never

IRRATIONAL EXPECTATIONS

This same rational and practical expectation (wanting affection from your partner) can be easily *mutated* into an irrational one. All you have to do is demand that you get affection, declare that it would be awful if you didn't get it, and condemn the person who failed to give it to you. When people think in this manner, bad, unhappy and disturbed feelings result.

The descriptions below show you why these "thinking styles" make little sense.

1. **Demandingness.** If you look for evidence to support the idea that your partner must give you affection, you won't find any. After all, why MUST your partner do anything you want. Your partner is an individual with the power NOT to meet your demands. It is best that you recognize that others will do what they want, not necessarily what you want. If you fail to accept this fact, you will continue to get angry when you don't get your way. We don't control the world around us, although most of us at one time or another have attempted to do so. Sooner or later we learn that such a feat is impossible.

2. **Awfulizing.** Another component of irrational thinking, awfulizing, makes little sense as well. First of all, when you awfulize you don't feel very good. Just pay attention to how you're feeling when you complain that things are awful. Observe how others feel when they are complaining in the same way. Are you or they happy and joyous? Hardly! It's easy to see how awfulizing violates the first rule of rational thinking by not getting you happiness. Second, there isn't any evidence to back up the idea that something is "awful". Most people think "awful" means 100% bad. If you really think about it, can anything be 100% bad, that is, without any redeeming quality whatsoever? Even feces has redeeming qualities associated with it—the nutrients available for plant growth when used as fertilizer. The use of the term "awful" can mean that something is worse than it is. Can anything be worse than it is at any particular point in time? Again, the answer is NO! Things can only be as bad as they are. It is better to think that things have differing degrees of unpleasantness.

3. **Condemnation.** The other component of irrational thinking, putting yourself or others down, occurs all too frequently. This kind of thinking occurs with no basis in fact and produces unhappiness. People who go around condemning themselves or others are not happy and don't appear to be having much fun. They are miser-

able. It is easy to see how the first rule of rationality (it gets you happiness) is absent. Is there evidence to support condemnation of self or others? There doesn't appear to be any. Here's the way I view it. The lack of perfection in each of us is well documented. I haven't found anyone who is perfect, at least not yet. That means we all make mistakes or choose the wrong path from time to time. Since this is the case, it doesn't make much sense to condemn ourselves or others when we act in accordance with this human trait. Condemning others for their mistakes or for not giving us what we want is about as smart as condemning an individual for having a nose, or blonde hair, or for being a certain height. Acknowledging and accepting our imperfections and the imperfections of others is the better alternative.

PRACTICAL AND IMPRACTICAL EXPECTATIONS

When we are preparing, sharing, and negotiating our expectations, it is a good idea that they be practical, as well as rational. An impractical expectation could be difficult to meet. For example, let's say you expect your mate to fly you to the moon for your next summer vacation. You <u>want</u> that to happen. You are not <u>demanding</u> that it happen, thinking it would be <u>awful</u> if it didn't happen or <u>condemning</u> your mate if he or she failed to provide it for you. According to the definitions above, you are thinking rationally. You <u>want</u> it to happen.

Given the near impossibility of space travel at this time, such an idea remains <u>impractical</u>, at least for now. You're better off altering this expectation to make it more practical or skipping it for now.

Because an expectation is <u>somewhat</u> out of reach doesn't mean that it should be automatically shelved. "Stretching" to reach a goal can lead to creative involvement making for active, exciting, and vital living. And remember, <u>if you fail</u>, it's hardly the end of the world, it doesn't make <u>you a failure</u>, and it doesn't mean that you can't try again.

GETTING DOWN TO WORK

Once you have clarified and defined your expectations and have determined that they are

37

CHAPTER 2 / What Do You Want to Get Out of This Relationship?

rational and practical, you and your partner can begin work on them. Of course your partner will help you continue the process of defining and clarifying, so when you finish, you will have a list of ideas that is mutually acceptable and workable. The following chapters will help you through this process. I predict you will begin to experience increased happiness as soon as you begin working on your expectations. And, as you continue the process and your expectations are actually being met, you will experience even greater levels of happiness. It may sound rather easy and simplistic. **It is simplistic, but it isn't easy.** It takes a lot of hard work and effort to make it happen and to have it continue happening. Loving feelings occur when you and your partner work hard meeting each other's expectations. **Working at love makes love happen.**

NOTES

Chapter 3

KEEPING YOUR EMOTIONS UNDER CONTROL

NOTES

Chapter 3

KEEPING YOUR EMOTIONS UNDER CONTROL

They came in, sat down. She looked at me, he didn't. She began to talk. He looked at her angrily, got up, and, as he left my office, slammed the door behind him. She said, "You just can't talk to him when he gets this way!"

This situation is likely to occur when emotions are *extreme and intense* and usually results in behavior that is equally extreme and intense. Left without avenues of effective communication, this couple has little chance for solving their problems.

EMOTIONAL STABILITY

HAVE PATIENCE!   *COOL DOWN!*   *TAKE IT EASY!*
DON'T GET SO UPSET!   *USE YOUR HEAD!*

These directives, easily given, are difficult to follow. However, they provide benefits for the individual who adopts them. People who take these ideas seriously find themselves experiencing greater *emotional stability*. Since emotional stability is a necessary precursor to *good decision-making*, and good decisions are more likely to bring you *happiness*, adopting ideas such as these is well worth it. Remember, emotional stability is not the elimination of emotion, but the control of excessive emotion.

Differences: Many people think that differences should not exist in an intimate, loving relationship, and that love should at least neutralize those differences. We become more vulnerable to emotional instability when we view differences this way. On the other hand, if you expect differences and appreciate the uniqueness of your partner, you'll be more tolerant toward whatever differences exist in your relationship. Tolerance and emotional stability go hand-in-hand.

Sharing Close Quarters: Living in close proximity with another person provides an unusual opportunity to examine the person and his/her expectations in minute detail. It's like having a magnifying glass and being able to continuously peer through it. You learn a lot, but not all you learn may be to your liking. The traits and characteristics you find may not fit your plan for happiness. When this happens you may become upset or downright disturbed (emotional instability). Unfortunately, excessive emotional disturbance is what we don't want. It interferes with good communication, problem-solving, and change, which is exactly what may be required if you are to get what you want out of the relationship. And, if you don't get what you want, sooner or later you will probably experience increasing levels of anger and hostility.

This chapter will describe methods to control and maintain emotional stability while you work on your expectations or on problem areas in your relationship. In the previous chapter, *Demandingness, Awfulizing* and *Condemnation* styles of thinking were discussed as elements of irrational expectations. These same styles of thinking produce *excessive negative* emotions. Remember, your excessive negative emotions (especially anger and hostility) are probably your most significant barriers to change. I have included additional readings, professional resources, and control techniques in the Appendices for you and your partner to use in case you find it difficult maintaining emotional stability. Don't despair if you experience a tough time controlling your emotions. This is one of the most difficult problems for just about everyone. As long as you and your partner are willing to work at it, your emotional stability will improve.

The Case of Alicia and Alan

Alicia continued to see me on a weekly basis despite the fact that Alan had left my office angrily three weeks before. He had decided not to return with her. She was interested in having a better relationship with Alan, despite his explosive outbursts, and wanted to learn to cope more effectively with them. Alicia told me of Alan's many other fine traits and characteristics and her wish not to give him up "just because of his temper".

I was surprised and glad when Alan accompanied Alicia to her next appointment. He apologized for his outburst weeks earlier. Alan acknowledged the destructiveness of his anger and expressed a desire to control it. I worked with him individually for over a month and a half before he felt he had gained enough control to begin marriage counseling.

The Central Problem Making Us Vulnerable to Emotional Instability: Humans tend to think "crookedly" and have to work very hard at thinking straight. We want things to go our way, and when we see this is not happening, we stubbornly refuse to adjust our thinking to the reality before us. We hang on to our demanding ideas and usually resort to intimidation in an attempt to get our way. When we demand things go our way over and over again we "condition" ourselves to believe the demand is legitimate. Because our brain works the way it does, we easily and effectively "brainwash" ourselves about our "crooked" thoughts. These new "conditioned" ideas come to mind easily, automatically and "naturally".

ANGER

When an idea has been established in our mind, we may demand that it occur or exist in reality. (Remember: something can exist as an idea in our mind without it existing in the real world.) When it does not occur or exist as we have demanded, we usually respond with ANGER, HOSTILITY, or RAGE. Soon after the anger comes BLAME, usually focused on those who have failed to respond to our demand. Sometimes we even blame ourselves for failing to get others to comply with our demand.   *Contribution*

What causes anger? Albert Ellis has identified the primary culprit to be demanding thinking. When followed by awfulizing and condemnation, anger is assured. In a pamphlet entitled The Nature of Disturbed Marital Relationships, Ellis characterizes the marital partners involved "as standing nose to nose demanding that the other give them or see it THEIR way". When you assume an "elitist, godly status" by declaring what is right and wrong for you as well as for others and condemn those who fail to meet your demand, you make yourself vulnerable to anger.

LOW FRUSTRATION TOLERANCE

Another way of looking at anger is to consider the concept of LOW FRUSTRATION TOLERANCE. When one believes "things" should be easy and they turn out to be difficult, anger and frustration result. Low frustration tolerance is another form of demanding that the world should be a certain way, your way!

SELF-RIGHTEOUSNESS

Self-righteousness is part of feeling angry. The underlying premise of the anger response is the belief that your ideas are absolutely right and your partner's ideas are absolutely wrong. When we think our ideas are right, we are likely to think that WE are right. People tend to transfer this "righteous" way of thinking to themselves, creating "self-righteousness". These shifts in thinking allow the anger created to be directed *at others*. It is not just their ideas that are wrong, *they* are wrong for thinking the way they do. We may even go so far as to prescribe punishment for their "wrongness".

This kind of thinking is distorted and absurd. None of us can be absolutely sure of anything in life, and we certainly can't be "absolutely sure that our ideas are absolutely right". Our ideas are plucked from a universe of possibilities and we settle for those that are most comfortable for us. This is a capricious and arbitrary process. The next unknown moment might very well prove our sacred true beliefs not to be so sacred and true. We are well advised to approach the beliefs we have acquired with humbleness, rather than with indignant self-righteousness.

GUILT

Another part of the anger response is self-blame or guilt. This happens when we *down ourselves* for getting angry. We incorrectly believe that we must not ever get angry (even though it is human), and *overly criticize ourselves* when we do. Instead of accepting our errors and trying to avoid them in the future, we blame ourselves, and do very little to correct problems by working hard to eliminate our imperfections. When uncorrected, imperfections continue to exist, problems begin to pile up and overwhelm us, creating guilt and depression. This can be disastrous for relationships.

CONTROLLING EXCESSIVE NEGATIVE EMOTIONS

<u>ABC's of Emotions</u>. Ellis uses a model that makes understanding our emotions a lot easier. Known as the "ABC model of emotions", it allows us to identify our feeling and behavioral responses to certain events, and enables us to identify the thoughts that precede them.

Many people think that our feelings are generated from things that happen in the world around us, rather than from within ourselves. Nothing could be further from the truth. **It is the way we think that creates our feelings.** That's right! The ideas, beliefs, points of view, philosophies and opinions that we rely on when events occur are primarily responsible for how we feel. This may sound too simple, but changing how we think changes how we feel. I want to say this one more time: **Challenging and changing our thoughts changes how we feel.** Let me explain in more detail, using the ABC model.

$$A \quad + \quad B \quad = \quad C$$

Events   Beliefs   Results

Some event, situation, or circumstance occurs at <u>A</u>. At <u>C</u>, we respond with a feeling and a behavior. If we fail to take into account <u>B</u>, we might conclude that <u>A</u> caused <u>C</u>. However, it's the <u>B</u>, your thinking and your beliefs about the <u>A</u> that caused the <u>C</u>. The following example might help explain this further.

A (event) = Your partner fails to keep a promise of having the car washed for your sister's wedding.

B (belief) = You tell yourself, "He should have kept his promise! How dare he fail to keep his promise to me? How could he do such a thing? I can't believe he forgot! He's such a jerk for forgetting!

C (result) = You feel angry and irritated and tell him off. You go to the wedding feeling this way and have a miserable time.

This example clearly shows the role of thinking (B) in producing the anger that is felt and the behavior that is chosen (C). Additional sets of ABC's can follow from the first one leading to a very complicated, confusing, and deteriorating set of circumstances. In other words, the C produced from the first A and B becomes the new A for the second set leading to a second B and C.

First Set: (first A) + B = C (first outcome)

Second Set: (first outcome becomes the second A) + B = C (second outcome)

Third Set: (second outcome becomes the third A) + B = C (third outcome)

Etc., etc., etc.

Let's return to the previous example and see how things can deteriorate.

FIRST SET
(Event) A = Partner fails to wash the car as promised.

(Thought) B = What a jerk! He should have remembered! I can't believe he forgot!

(Result) C = You tell him off and go to the wedding feeling angry.

SECOND SET
(Event) A = You tell him off and go to the wedding feeling angry.

(Thought) B = I should be having fun and I'm not. If it weren't for him I would be! He's ruined my day and my sister's wedding.

(Result) C = He asks you to dance and you refuse. You excuse yourself and go to the restroom and cry. You miss the cutting of the wedding cake.

THIRD SET
(Event) A = You miss the cutting of the wedding cake.

(Thought) B = I can't believe I missed my sister cutting the wedding cake! I've missed out on everything today! If only he hadn't been so irresponsible. What a louse!

(Result) C = You refuse to talk with him for the next two weeks and see everything he does as irresponsible.

Knowing that these "strings" of ABC's occur should help you to understand how things can deteriorate quickly, leaving you upset and in a state of confusion. It emphasizes the importance of challenging the thoughts leading to anger as soon as it happens - so you can control your emotions immediately and choose behaviors that lead to solutions, not angry behaviors that cause more problems.

Exercise: Identifying the B

Instructions: Try to identify the thoughts that precede the emotions in the situations presented below. Remember to look for the thoughts that are demanding, awfulizing, and condemning. (Answers found at the end of the chapter.)

A (Situation): You finish raking the leaves in your yard, but before you have a chance to bag them, the wind blows them all back.

C (Response): You feel very angry, throw your rake to ground, and stomp off and yell at the kids.

B (Thoughts): _How DARE THE WIND BLOW ; THIS ISN'T FAIR_

A (Situation): Your partner announces that she/he wants to spend some time alone, without you, and suggests spending the weekend at a motel hours away.

C (Response): You experience anxiety and fear, and try to get him/her to tell you what is wrong.

B (Thoughts): _____

A (Situation): A friend expresses anger toward you for not remembering a luncheon engagement.

C (Response): You are shocked and then feel sad and depressed.

B (Thoughts): _____

The next step using the ABC model is to challenge the B. You challenge your ideas simply by asking WHY YOUR THOUGHTS ARE TRUE. We'll call these steps "D" and "E". Let's do that using the example of the partner who forgot to have the car washed for the wedding.

B (belief)	=	"He should have kept his promise!"
D (challenge)	=	"WHY should he have kept his promise?"
E (answer)	=	"He doesn't have to keep his promise, although it would be better for me if he had!"

B (belief)	=	"How dare he fail to keep his promise to me?"
D (challenge)	=	"WHY can't he fail to keep his promise to me?"
E (answer)	=	"He can fail to keep his promise to me, even though I wished he hadn't!"

B (belief)	=	"How could he do such a thing?"
D (challenge)	=	"WHY can't he do what he did?"
E (answer)	=	"He can do such a thing; he controls what he does, not me!"

B (belief)	=	"I can't believe he forgot!"
D (challenge)	=	"WHY can't he forget?"
E (answer)	=	"He can forget; after all, he's human!"

B (belief)	=	"He's such a jerk for forgetting!"
D (challenge)	=	"HOW does it make him a jerk for forgetting?"
E (answer)	=	"It doesn't make him a jerk for forgetting; what it makes him is human!"

If you take the time to ask why your beliefs are true and look for answers, you are likely to curb or even prevent anger and keep the situation from deteriorating. This is an important aspect of living sanely and happily with another person.

Now that you have moderated your emotional response by challenging and changing the anger causing beliefs, you can more easily explore and formulate a plan of action.

Again, using the previous example.

> **C (Old Result):** You feel angry and irritated and tell him off. You go to the wedding feeling this way and have a miserable time.

> **F (New Result):** You feel only mildly irritated and tell him you are disappointed at not having a clean car for the wedding. He apologizes and hopes it won't spoil the wedding. You agree to enjoy yourself despite the condition of the car.

Controlling your emotions can be further facilitated through the use of additional techniques and methods. These techniques are discussed in more detail in the chapters and appendices that follow. You may wish to read these sections of the book before proceeding, especially if you anticipate difficulty controlling your emotions. The essential thing to keep in mind is that you are responsible for your own emotions. If you take the time to identify, challenge, change and practice thinking in ways that moderate your emotions, you will be more successful in negotiating your relationship and finding happiness.

Answers to the Exercise: Identifying the B

1st Situation. Blown leaves followed by anger.

"I spent all this time raking these leaves. This isn't fair. How could such a thing happen to me? I can't stand it when things don't go my way! Damn it! Things never go my way!"

2nd Situation. Separation from partner followed by anxiety.

"What if something is wrong? What if she/he is planning to leave me? That would be awful! I couldn't stand to live if I didn't have her/him around! What if I can't convince her/him to stay? I've got to try!"

3rd Situation. Anger from friend followed by depression.

"Oh, no! What's wrong with me? I shouldn't have forgotten! This is unforgivable! What good am I if I can't keep my commitments to my friends?"

NOTES

Chapter 4

NEGOTIATION: THE ART OF COMPROMISE AND CHANGE

NOTES

Chapter 4

NEGOTIATION:
THE ART OF COMPROMISE AND CHANGE

DIFFERENCES

Nowhere are individual differences more evident than in a relationship. Each interaction serves to emphasize individual personality traits and may even magnify them. Due to the individualistic nature of human existence, differences are the norm rather than the exception. We are separate biologies with thoughts, feelings, and behaviors that are uniquely our own. We are all different and experience life from our own perspective. Differences present special problems for relationships.

If differences are viewed as alien and threatening to a relationship, the conclusion is simple: eliminate them. Many people believe that if differences are allowed to exist in a relationship, certain events will ultimately follow. Predictions include a lessening of intimacy, a loss of love, and eventually, termination of the relationship. In this case, determined effort to rid a relationship of differences is favored. This view most likely has its roots based in a widely accepted romantic notion: *creating a relationship with another person **means** creating 'oneness' with that person and sacrificing one's individuality*—for love, of course.

Actually, the opposite is true. Giving up your individuality and attempting to create this mythical "oneness" with the other person is pure fantasy and one of the most absurd romantic notions ever to have been created by humans. I, along with others, believe it is critical to give up this idea if you are to find happiness with a partner. The teachings of Kahlil Gibran illustrate the positive aspects of differences.

Dr. George
eulogy

From <u>The Prophet</u> . . . . "Then Almitra spoke
again and said, And what of Marriage, master?
And he answered saying:
You were born together, and together you shall be forevermore.
You shall be together when the white wings of death scatter your days.

Ay, you shall be together even in the silent memory of God.
But let there be spaces in your togetherness,
And let the winds of the heavens dance between you.

Love one another, but make not a bond of love:
Let it rather be a moving sea between the shores of your souls.
Fill each other's cup but drink not from one cup.
Give one another of your bread but eat not from the same loaf.
Sing and dance together and be joyous, but let each one of you be alone,
Even as the strings of a lute are alone though they quiver with the same music.

Give your hearts, but not into each other's keeping.
For only the hand of Life can contain your hearts.
And stand together yet not too near together:
For the pillars of the temple stand apart,
And the oak tree and the cypress grow not in each other's shadow."

CHANGE

Whether expected or unexpected, change created by the individuals involved or by events outside their control is omnipresent. Change is difficult and many individuals seek to avoid it if they can. However, change can also provide us with unusual opportunities for growth when it is embraced rather than avoided. Learning to negotiate and compromise will allow you to face change with more confidence. This chapter will discuss negotiating skills and show you how to use them.

NEGOTIATING AND COMPROMISE

Differences and Change, two dynamic life factors affecting your relationship and your happiness, require negotiating and compromise. Negotiation should, if properly done, lead to "agreements" that are mutually acceptable and generate happiness for the two people involved. The "agreements" should be reviewed periodically and revised in response to changing conditions (situations, people, and desires). In this sense, agreements are rarely final.

Cautionary Note 1:

Care should be exercised throughout the entire negotiating process not to attribute arbitrary meaning to your partner's behavior (you defining your partner's behavior). Good communication techniques are designed to help you avoid making this common error. We want you to define and give meaning to your behavior and we want your partner to define and give meaning to his/her behavior. This point will be discussed later in this chapter.

Cautionary Note 2:

It is also important, as pointed out earlier, to <u>accept</u> your partner with <u>all</u> of his/her positive and negative traits and characteristics, while reserving the right to like or dislike those traits and characteristics. Assertive negotiation will result in personal happiness, provided you refrain from anger and blame. Treating your partner with respect will likely lead to an obvious relationship benefit—respectful treatment by your partner.

Cautionary Note 3:

A person who compromises, explores, gives explanations, and asks for clarification will experience more success in the negotiating process. On the other hand, one who surrenders, withdraws, criticizes, gives in, pressures, threatens, or evades issues is likely to give less than a satisfactory performance.

Cautionary Note 4:

Personality traits resulting in the failure of or the inability to negotiate may indicate the need for psychotherapy. It may be to everyone's advantage to wait and negotiate relationship issues after therapy has been completed.

COMMUNICATION

Communication is the lifeblood of the negotiating process, allowing for compromise, understanding, and agreements. Communication occurs in verbal and non-verbal form, but the goal in either case is to convey understanding. This is a very complicated process vulnerable to misunderstanding. The information that follows will be helpful to you in using effective communication to increase understanding.

THE COMMUNICATION PROCESS

When a person has an idea or message to share, an <u>encoding</u> procedure is begun. It involves taking the idea you have and putting it into words and/or gestures so that your partner can see or hear your idea. Once your message is received, a <u>decoding</u> procedure is initiated by your partner giving substance to the message. This encoding and decoding process, if left to stand alone without some form of clarification, will almost always result in misunderstanding and a breakdown in the communication process.

<u>Cautionary Note 5</u>:

> Our thinking and the expression of our thoughts become so automatic that most of the time we don't have to "stop and think" in order to communicate. However, sometimes it is a very good idea to pause to make decisions about **how** we want to communicate before we do it. It reduces mistakes. Removing your thoughts from your mind by writing them down gives you a better chance to evaluate them. This applies to WHAT you are saying and HOW you say it. Your tone of voice or a raised eyebrow may convey a meaning to your partner, not intended. Remember, gestures count. The following exercise may help you appreciate the importance of this fact.

Exercise: Non-Verbal Meanings

Write down an idea you wish to communicate to your partner in the space provided below. Any idea will do, like what you want to do in the next hour, or the kind of car you like, or what happened to you today. Go ahead and write it down. Be brief.

_____

_____

_____

_____

_____

_____

Now communicate the idea exactly as you have written it, but with a sarcastic tone in your voice, or with a cocked eyebrow, or with a frown on your face. After communicating with your partner, ask him/her what you meant by what you said and see if the meaning gathered is different from the meaning written above. This exercise should show you the importance of non-verbal messages sent along with the actual words. Repeat the exercise having your partner send a message with you as the listener.

Since people easily and frequently interpret similar events differently, a great deal of effort may be required to uncover the intended meaning. If you and your partner are willing to work hard to clarify the meaning of messages, you stand a very good chance of being successful communicators.

The following describes how our thinking (cognitive processing) works when an event or communication occurs.

1. Something happens or is communicated (stimulus).
2. We perceive the stimulus using one or more of our senses (seeing, hearing, smelling, tasting, or touching).
3. We define and describe the stimulus to ourselves using language (words). We tell ourselves what it is.
4. Then we infer certain traits or characteristics about the stimulus. We tell ourselves what it is like.

Keep in mind that all of this happens before we *evaluate* the stimulus (decide whether it is "good" or "bad"). With so many steps involved in the cognitive and communication process, it is easy to see how errors can and do occur. When you add another person to this already complicated process, the potential for misunderstanding increases dramatically.

Now that you have a better understanding of the complicated communication process and the enormous capacity for error, I'm sure you see the value of using various techniques and methods to minimize error. However, 100% error-free communication is not very likely. None of us is perfect. Don't get discouraged if you make mistakes; keep trying and you'll get better.

A COMMUNICATION METHOD

I use a three step communication technique to help reduce communication errors and increase the level of understanding between partners. The procedure goes like this:

1. Person "A" sends a communication to Person "B". *(Communication)*
2. Person "B" repeats the communication to Person "A". *(Feedback)*
3. Person "A" indicates the accuracy of the feedback to Person "B". *(Confirmation)*

If positive confirmation is received, the communicators can be relatively sure that each knows the content or structure of the message, that it has been accurately communicated and received. If positive confirmation is not given, the message can be restated and sent again, repeating the above steps until positive confirmation is received.

Once the content of the message has been communicated and received accurately, it is important to make sure there is a clear understanding of the *meaning* of the message. Further communication steps between the two communicators, "A" and "B", will be necessary to accomplish this task.

1. Person "A" defines what the message means *by illustrating with behavioral descriptions that are observable:*

> He/she may say, "When you yell and your face turns red, I get very frightened. And, when I get frightened, I start sweating and want to run away!"
> Person "A" can also provide reasons for the feelings and behavior. He/she may say, "Here's why I feel the way I do" and then list the reasons.
>
> Then, person "B" may respond by asking person "A" for further behavioral descriptions or reasons.

Take your time with this step. Make sure you know what you and your partner are talking about!

2. After the observable behaviors and/or reasons are explored using the three-step method (presentation, feedback, and confirmation), *discussion can occur where individual opinions and views are shared.* Debate is encouraged; however, it is very important to follow the advice and direction given in Chapter 3, "Keeping Your Emotions Under Control". Debating without excessive negative emotion will yield good results. Make sure meanings are explored and understood. After you have debated, shared your ideas, listened to your partner's ideas, then go on to step three.

3. The final step in the process is called integration, *when you and your partner evaluate what has been discussed and come to some agreement.* This step is necessary in order to close on the communication, even if it is only to agree to talk about it at another time. If you are not able to come to terms, you may agree to disagree. That may sound strange, but it is a very logical outcome when you both feel strongly about an issue and feel your particular point of view is valid. Agreeing to disagree is, in fact, integrating the decision into the mix of the relationship. However, if "agreeing to disagree" is determined to be detrimental to the relationship, then it is advisable to get back to the negotiation process and attempt to reach agreement.

APPRECIATION / RESENTMENT SESSIONS

A communication exercise called "Appreciation/Resentment" provides a structure for the use of the four-stage communication process (Confirming Content, Defining Meaning, Discussing Perspectives and Integrating Ideas). Try it with your partner using an issue the two of you are interested in integrating. It can be something you *appreciate* or something you *resent* concerning the relationship or each other. When you feel comfortable with the use of this technique, you can go on to discuss additional topics/issues that have significance for you. The step-by-step outline and example that follows should help you with your first try.

1. **Initiation or Presentation Stage (Confirming Content)**

    a. Person "A" communicates an idea to Person "B".

        Example: "I don't like it when you smoke, especially when you do it in front of the children!"

b. Person "B" repeats what was communicated from Person "A".

> **Example**: "What I heard you say was that you don't like it when I smoke, especially when I do it in front of the children."

c. Person "A" confirms the feedback to Person "B".

> **Example**: "Yes, that's right, that's what I said!"

2. **Explanation of Reasons Stage (Defining Meaning)**

a. Person "A" presents reasons for her dislike to Person "B".

> **Example**: "The reasons I dislike it so are that it smells, it make me cough, it costs too much money, it'll ruin your health, and it sets a bad example for the kids."

b. Person "B" gives feedback to Person "A".

> **Example**: "What I understand you to say is that it smells, costs too much, and will set a bad example for Mike and Sue. Is that correct?"

c. Person "A" corrects the misunderstanding with a restatement of the reasons.

> **Example**: "Well, dear, you got part of it correct, but not all of it. Actually, what I said, in addition to it costing too much, smelling, and setting a bad example for the kids, was that it is bad for your health and makes me cough. Do you understand?"

d. Person "B" restates with additional feedback.

> **Example**: "Now I've got it. It smells, sets a bad example for the kids, makes you cough, costs too much, and you believe it'll be bad for my health. Right?"

e. Person "A" gives confirmation to Person "B".

> **Example**: "Right!"

3. **Discussion/Debate Stage (Discussing Perspectives)**

Either Person "A" or "B" can begin by expressing their opinions/views/beliefs concerning each of the reasons given. This section has less structure because of the legitimate variety of views that humans have. Many subjects are simply "a matter of personal taste". Therefore, it is very important to allow views to be expressed openly, keeping in mind that you don't have to agree with them. It is also important to keep in mind that your partner may have some valuable points to share. This can lead to a reassessment of your position and an important change for you and the relationship.

Note: (The following example does not represent an exhaustive discussion of this particular topic. It is intended to provide guidance to the reader in the practical use of this technique.)

Example:

"B" - "What do you mean, my smoking causes you to cough?"

"A" - "That's right! When I am around you or anyone else who has been smoking, I have noticed that I tend to cough."

"B" - "Well, maybe there is something wrong with you. I can't imagine that my smoking is affecting you that much! Maybe you should go ask your doctor about it before you blame it on me."

"A" - "Wait a minute, I'm not blaming it on you, I'm blaming it on your smoking. But I see what you mean, maybe I should go see my doctor about it. It is time that I have my annual physical exam anyway."

"A" - "Okay, but what about the bad example it sets for our children? You would have to agree that it doesn't set the best example?"

"B" - "Well, I'm not so sure!"

"A" - "Come on, psychologists are pretty certain that kids learn a great deal from their parents. They say that kids use their parents for 'role models' and adopt many of their same habits, good and bad!"

"B" - "Well, I agree that I don't think that I want my kids smoking, now or in the future. And, if what you say is true, maybe I should be more discreet, especially when the kids are around. Could you get me some of the information you've been reading about, you know, the stuff you said you read about role models?"

"A" - "Sure, I'd be happy to, anything to get you to think about the possibility of stopping!"

(This example only explored two of the five items raised by Person "A". The other three items should be discussed in the same manner with appropriate follow-up.)

4. **Resolution Stage (Integrating Ideas)**

Person "A" and Person "B" attempt to come to terms.

Example:

"A" - "Well, we've talked about your smoking quite a bit in the last two weeks. What have you decided?"

"B" - "A number of good points have been made, but smoking does give me quite a bit of pleasure! I would be willing to cut down by one-half and not to smoke around the children at all. Is that acceptable to you?"

"A" - "I would prefer that you quit altogether, but what you are willing to do is better than what you were doing before. I'm willing to try it out for a couple of months if you are. But I want to discuss this again."

"B" - "Okay, let's give it a whirl!"

Now that you understand the procedure, try it. Don't be overly concerned if it is awkward; most new tools are until you have had enough practice enabling you to feel "natural" using it. When you have practiced enough, the process will flow more easily and actually begin to feel "natural" when you communicate.

The above procedure contains many elements considered important in solving problems.

1. Problems/issues/concerns are stated clearly and concisely.
2. Reasons are presented backing-up particular points of view.
3. Reactions are shared.
4. Solutions are considered and resources explored.
5. A plan is agreed upon and carried out.
6. Agreement is reached to assess the results sometime in the future.

There will be plenty of opportunity to practice as you and your partner continue to explore the expectation process. Working at it is the key element in achieving success. The reward will be the love you are seeking.

NOTES

Chapter 5

LISTING YOUR SPECIFIC
EXPECTATIONS AND
DEFINING EXACTLY
WHAT YOU MEAN

NOTES

Chapter 5

LISTING YOUR SPECIFIC EXPECTATIONS AND DEFINING EXACTLY WHAT YOU MEAN

You are now ready to start listing the expectations you have for a partner. This chapter will help you compile your own unique list and give you some idea of the expectations that others have created. Of course, you are not limited to these ideas, they are simply there to remind you of the many options available. Developing a clear idea of what you want is one of the first steps in finding happiness in a relationship.

Expectations are a matter of personal preference, so now is the time for you to assert your individuality. You, your happiness, and your unique way of getting it is all that matters at this point. There will be ample time for modification and compromise later. Right now, give yourself priority and list all the things in a relationship that are important for your happiness.

Of course, there are some limitations worth considering. Try to make sure your expectations are *rational and practical.* Remember, a *rational* expectation is a desire that is thought about in a preferential manner rather than in a demanding manner. When you think of it in a demanding manner, you transform it into an irrational expectation.

> A client I recently worked with kept getting exceedingly upset at her husband for not spending more time with the children. Upon further investigation, I discovered my client had been thinking along demanding lines. Her thoughts were: "He must spend more time with the children!" In addition, she thought that it was awful if he didn't, adding more fuel to her emotional fire. Further, she damned him for doing a poor job with the children. When she revised her expectation to a more preferential style, she felt less disturbed (in this case less angry) and was able to approach him in a less hostile manner. Her new preferential thought went something like this. "I prefer he spend more time with the children. I don't like it that he doesn't, but I can stand it. He's not all bad! I think I'll talk with him about this tomorrow." When she calmed herself down, she was better able to discuss her concerns and urge him to make some desired changes in his fathering style.

It is also important for your expectations to be *practical*. They should be within or just outside reach. In other words, practical expectations should be reachable with a reasonable amount of effort within a reasonable amount of time. Obviously, the decision of what is "reasonable" will differ from person to person and from situation to situation. You and your partner are the best judge of what is reasonable.

One way of establishing reasonableness and practicality is to determine the likelihood of something happening. Try to determine if it is *more or less* likely to happen. This is the "probability of occurrence" method. If something is more likely to occur, then it is more likely to be practical and reasonable. Expectations that are *very unlikely* (say 10 percent chance of occurring) probably should be eliminated from your list.

Exercise A: Identifying Your Expectations

For the many couples I have seen in marriage counseling over the years, there are just as many unique sets of expectations. However, at the same time, there are many similarities in expectations selected and considered important in a relationship. In the list that follows, see if there are expectations (traits, characteristics and behaviors of a partner) that are important to you and your happiness. Check those items off. Do this without thinking about it too long, check it off if you "feel" it is important to you. We will consider each item in more detail later. Some additional blank spaces have been left at the end for you to list items that have not been included in the list. (Note: "Expectations" as used throughout this book means "wishes, preferences, and desires", not "absolute demands or requirements".

_____ Warm and affectionate
_____ Cooperative with household tasks
_____ Confident
_____ Mature and self-supportive
_____ Sense of humor
_____ Emotionally supportive, gives encouragement
_____ Honest and truthful
_____ Financial partnership/responsible

_____ Sexually inclined and interested
_____ Optimistic
_____ Interested in activities outside relationship
_____ Allows for privacy and freedom
_____ Wants children
_____ Career oriented
_____ Interacts socially
_____ Shares control of the relationship
_____ Communicates easily
_____ Makes adjustments and is flexible
_____ Attentive to others
_____ Supportive of growth in others
_____ Is physically fit
_____ Physically attractive
_____ Respects others
_____ Shares similar religious views
_____ Shares similar political views
_____ Assertive
_____ Relaxed, not tense
_____ Open to new ideas
_____ Expresses feelings
_____ Commitment oriented

_____ _____

_____ _____

_____ _____

_____ _____

_____ _____

<u>Reminder.</u> This list does not represent a complete set of expectations. It is intended to help you identify areas of concern and interest frequently found in a relationship. Additional listings can be found in Appendix E.

DEFINING YOUR EXPECTATIONS

Now that you have identified those areas that you feel are important to your happiness, your remaining task is to define what you <u>mean</u>. Providing the meaning of an expectation is a critical step in the communication process. Without it your partner would have to guess at what you mean. This book is designed to take the guesswork out of finding love and happiness.

When it comes to defining each item, use "behaviorally specific" definitions. **Describe what you would need to <u>SEE</u> your partner <u>DO</u> in order for you to know that your partner was meeting your expectation.** I can't emphasize this point too much. This is extremely critical to the whole process and, without it, may lead to an unsuccessful outcome.

> Your partner needs to convert your "expectation idea" into behaviors and you need to see what your partner is doing in order for you to relate it to your "expectation idea".

Being behaviorally specific is the only way I know to have the two of you be able to "observe and verify".

> Let's take the first item in the list of expectations, warm and affectionate. Let's say you consider this very important in a relationship. You tell your partner you want him/her to be warm and affectionate but give no explanation of what you mean (no definition). Your partner may be confused and give you what he/she thinks is warmth and affectionate behavior. You may get the opposite of what you want. Your partner doesn't know what you want because you haven't defined it. If you define it by telling your partner what behaviors represent warmth and affection, the confusion will clear up, and so will your chances of getting what you want.

> Example: "I would like you to hold my hand when we go for a walk, give me a hug when there isn't any special reason to, smile and greet me when we see each other after working all day long, and tell me you love me."

This is a clear and specific definition of warm and affectionate behavior. It would be unlikely for a partner to make mistakes (because of not knowing) after this definition was given.

Example No. 1

When asked to do this exercise, a client of mine came up with the following list of expectations and definitions for each. Look it over to see how the definitions are stated. Note how specific and behavioral they are. Keep in mind that this is just one person's view of what is preferred in a partner. Yours may differ substantially.

1. **Perception of Himself.**
   Self-confident.
   > Does not make self-deprecating remarks.
   > Is not overly critical of self.
   > Does not unreasonably deprecate or criticize others.
   > Considers himself worthy of other's respect.
   Is reasonably satisfied with his accomplishments.
   > Speaks with pride of his accomplishments.
   > Does not belittle or ignore accomplishments of others.
   > Believes he deserves rewards for his labors.
   Independent.
   > Is capable of handling day to day affairs alone.
   > Does not unnecessarily lean on others.
   Assertive.
   > Does not permit others to take advantage of him.

2. **Life Style.**
   Time management.
   > Can set goals and accomplish them without procrastination.
   Fitness.
   > Eats and exercises wisely.
   > Is at desirable weight.
   > Is not frequently ill.
   > Does not use tobacco.
   > Uses alcohol moderately.
   Relaxation.
   > Allows self adequate time for relaxation and recreation.

3. **Intellect.**

    Articulate.

        Expresses ideas precisely.

        Understands nuances of expression.

        Uses proper diction.

    Curiosity and growth.

        Pursues interests beyond self and job.

        Reads, watches movies, sees plays and analyzes same.

    Flexibility.

        Is open to new ideas.

    Aesthetics.

        Is involved in and pursues the arts.

4. **Emotions.**

    Love.

        Verbalizes love.

        Demonstrates love.

    Anger.

        Expresses anger when appropriate.

        Expresses anger in appropriate manner.

        Doesn't hang on to anger once it's expressed.

    Stability.

        Is pretty much the same person every time I see him.

        Can compartmentalize problems and keep them from spilling out in other areas.

    Happiness.

        Prefers happiness to unhappiness.

        Makes conscious choices to assure his happiness.

5. **Sexuality.**

    Frequency.

        Enjoys sex often.

        Arranges plans to enjoy sex often.

    Quality.

        Is fun and tender and passionate and sensual.

As a sexual partner.

    Is physically attractive to me.

    Is physically attracted to me.

    Is sexually confident.

    Is sexually competent.

    Enjoys different techniques.

6. **His Family's Relationship to Me.**

Mutual respect and affection verbalized.

Mutual respect and affection demonstrated.

Give their blessings to a continuing relationship between him and me.

7. **Relationship with Others.**

Immediate family.

    Is emotionally supportive.

    Offers guidance when necessary.

Co-workers.

    Respects those who work for him and for whom he works.

Interpersonal relationships.

    Insists that waiters, sales clerks, etc. perform to his satisfaction.

My family and close friends.

    Respects and defends them.

    Likes and is liked by my son.

8. **Relationship with Me.**

Respect.

    Listens to my point of view even when it is divergent from his own.

    Does not attack my standards or principles.

    Is willing to discuss differences.

    Isn't "knee-jerk" defensive when differences arise.

Love.

    Verbalizes loving feelings.

    Demonstrates loving feelings.

Commitment.
> Is capable of making commitments.
> Is willing to make commitments.
> Is able to sustain a commitment.
> Follows through on promises.

Common interests.
> Shares interest in dancing, nature, fishing, etc.

Possessiveness.
> Is not unreasonably jealous.
> Trusts me.

Supportive.
> Verbalizes support for my goals.
> Expends energy to help me reach my goals.

Even though this represents a very extensive list of expectations, there are a number of definitions that could have been more specifically and behaviorally defined. "Assertiveness" was defined as "not permitting others to take advantage of him". What behavior would be considered "not permitting others to take advantage of him"? This is not clear and further clarification is necessary. An example of a clarifying statement is found below:

> "by standing one's ground even though there is a risk involved, by saying no when one wants to say no, or yes when one wants to say yes…by not making decisions when someone else is urging you to do so and you are not ready to make one…by indicating that you'll think it over and get back to them".

This lends clarity to the expectation. The more specific you are, the better.

Example No. 2

Another client provided the following list of expectations:

1. **Finances**
> Comfortable lifestyle

Willing to spend on home, entertainment

Recreation within means

Some savings or investment

Reserves credit cards for major or special purchases to be paid in full at billing date saving credit line for emergency use

2. **Fun**

Things in common to do

Willing to do things, visit friends, play golf, take the day off, make a great meal

Shows enjoyment, gets involved in activities, smiles a lot, suggests repeating event

3. **Family**

Family oriented

Keeps contact with family

Willingly attends family functions

Wants children sooner or later, depending on finances

4. **Friendship**

Someone I can say anything to without feeling silly

Someone who will talk with me

Someone who will ask my help

Someone who I would ask for help

Shares thoughts, opinions, dreams without hesitation

Accepts differences

5. **Intelligent**

Able to speak well

Reads something other than magazines

Has and uses common sense

Has and uses mature judgment

6.. **Honesty**

Open about thoughts and opinions

Can be trusted with a secret, not to be repeated or used against me

Reliable

Someone I can respect in action

Responsible

7. **Confidence and Self-Assured**

Asks my opinion, but doesn't rely on it

Able to disagree without being angry

Doesn't take it personally if I read, or take a bath, or shop instead of joining him

Has own interests with or without me

8. **Sensitive and Kind**

To others' feelings

Doesn't tell "cat stories"

A word of sympathy on a lousy day or when I've had a bad experience

Congratulations on an accomplishment

Supports an ambition

Exercise B: Defining Your Expectations

In the following exercise list and define your expectations (desires and preferences). Take the items you checked above, place them in the left column, then add *specific and behavioral* definitions in the right column. If you need more space, continue the exercise on additional sheets of paper. Remember, <u>be specific and describe behaviors</u> when you define the expectation.

Expectation   Behavioral Definition

_____   _____

                               _____

                               _____

                               _____

                               _____

Expectation	Behavioral Definition
_____	_____
	_____
	_____
	_____
	_____
_____	_____
	_____
	_____
	_____
	_____
_____	_____
	_____
	_____
	_____
	_____
_____	_____
	_____
	_____
	_____
	_____
_____	_____
	_____
	_____

Look your list and definitions over carefully after you have completed this exercise. If necessary, redefine or include more behaviorally specific descriptions to add clarity to your list. If you have gotten this far, you are well on your way to discussing these concerns with your partner. But not quite yet! There is still some more individual work for you to do. Let's go on to Chapter 6.

NOTES

Chapter 6

THE IMPORTANCE OF YOUR EXPECTATIONS, SCORING YOUR PARTNER'S PERFORMANCE AND SETTING PRIORITIES

NOTES

Chapter 6

THE IMPORTANCE OF YOUR EXPECTATIONS, SCORING YOUR PARTNER'S PERFORMANCE AND SETTING PRIORITIES

Now that you have completed the task of identifying and defining your expectations, you are ready to determine the **importance** of each. You will also determine **how well** or to what extent your expectations are currently being met and how satisfied you are as a result. Both ratings are important personal estimates that will help you evaluate your current happiness in the relationship and its potential for future happiness. There is an additional advantage when you create **"importance"** and **"performance"** scores. These scores will enable you to identify and target specific areas of concern. Consequently, the time spent in the negotiating process is likely to be more productive.

Determining the Importance of an Expectation

Determining the importance of an expectation helps you more clearly communicate the complexities of your expectations. Since expectations vary in importance, communicating those variations to your partner is important. In addition, our attitudes, personal tastes and unique preferences change. This process should be repeated periodically, updating your expectations. More on this later.

Importance Rating Scale. The scale that will be used is a simple 9-point rating scale that converts "importance" into numbers. We will assume an expectation included on your list has some degree of importance or it wouldn't be there. Therefore, the scale will run from 1 to 9. The meaning of each number is represented below:

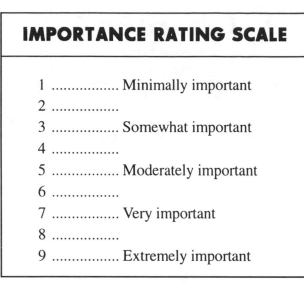

When you weigh the importance of each expectation, consider each one separately. Several of them may receive the same score because they are equally important to you. That's perfectly okay. Remember, your scores are a matter of personal preference and represent the value you uniquely assign to each.

Example: Importance Ratings of Ten Expectations

Expectation #1	7
Expectation #2	5
Expectation #3	8
Expectation #4	9
Expectation #5	3
Expectation #6	8
Expectation #7	3
Expectation #8	7
Expectation #9	7
Expectation #10	2

As you can see in the example above, some of the expectations received the same rating and the rest of the expectations received different ratings. These ratings reflect the unique view of the person doing the rating and represent important information to be shared.

Exercise: Importance Rating

Retrieve the list of expectations and the definitions you completed in the exercise in the last chapter. Go over each one and assign the number that best represents its degree of importance to you.

I would strongly suggest you use index cards to record and store all information for each expectation. That includes the expectation, the definition, the important score and other items described later in this chapter. Failure to put the information on index cards may result in losing information or becoming confused when trying to keep track of the expectations you and your partner have selected. Or, you may wish to store the information in your computer and then retrieve it when you need to review or use the information in the negotiating process. Develop a one page form and enter the information for each expectation. When you need it for the negotiating process, print it out.

Place the number representing the importance score after the expectation and definition description.

<u>Expectation</u>	Provide emotional support and encouragement
<u>Definition</u>	Ask about my plans for growth and development. Listen to my ideas, concerns and problems. Provide suggestions and offer solutions. Agree to make concessions if my plans dictate.
<u>Importance Score</u>	7

Giving this expectation an importance score of "7" communicates a message to your partner that emotional support and encouragement is **very important** to you. In most instances your partner could decide to meet your expectation with just this information. However, an additional piece of information will make the effort even more worthwhile.

DETERMINING THE MINIMUM ACCEPTABLE LEVEL OF PERFORMANCE SCORE

Now is the time to establish the "bottom line" for your partner's performance in meeting your expectations.

> *The "bottom line" is entirely arbitrary, defined by you and based on how much you want an expectation to occur.*

You should give this part of the process careful and thoughtful consideration. When establishing your MALP (Minimum Acceptable Level of Performance) you communicate a very important piece of information to your partner about each expectation -

> **where your happiness ends and your unhappiness begins.**

You are telling your partner that you will be satisfied with his/her performance, as long as it remains above this point. If your partner's performance drops below this point, your partner will know that you will be dissatisfied. The further the performance is above the MALP, the greater your satisfaction, the further it falls below the MALP, the greater your dissatisfaction.

The best way to express this "point" is to convert it to a number and have it represent "the percentage of the time the expectation is met" (0 to 100 percent).

Exercise: Determining the "MALP" for Your Partner's Performance

Ask yourself if you would be satisfied with getting your expectation met 100% of the time. This means your partner gives you what you want all the time. Obviously, the answer would be yes. Next, ask yourself if you would be satisfied with getting what you wanted 95% of the time. Each time you say "yes" continue reducing the performance score by 5% and continue to ask the question. When you finally answer "no, I would not be satisfied with my partner's performance at this level", you have reached the "dissatisfaction" range. Return to the percentage that immediately preceded your "no" answer. This will be your MALP score. Write this score on your index card.

DETERMINING THE PERFORMANCE OF YOUR PARTNER

Next, consider your partner's performance: what percentage of the time is your partner meeting a specific expectation. Again, give careful and thoughtful consideration to this estimate. In this step you are going to estimate your partner's "expectation meeting behavior" based on a recall of recent behavior. I would suggest you measure what you have <u>seen</u> and <u>heard</u> from your partner in the <u>last six months</u> and write it down. I selected six months as the "review period" to avoid short-term variations in behavior that may be misleading. Looking at your partner's behavior over six months is likely to give you a more reliable estimate.

Remember, the higher the performance, the happier you will be. If your partner's performance is high (let's say your expectations are met 85% of the time) you will be happy 85% of the time. Conversely, if the performance is low (your expectations are met only 20% of the time), you will experience happiness only 20% of the time.

The MALP "point" established by you previously will determine whether you are satisfied or dissatisfied with your partner's performance.

> Note: You may not expect your partner to meet an expectation very often. In such situations, your MALP score obviously would be low. Example: You expect your partner to call you 10% of the time when away from home on business trips. Calls are made to you 20% of the time. Despite the "low performance" (20% of the time), you would be satisfied because the performance is above the MALP of 10%.

PERFORMANCE AND SATISFACTION RANGES

I have developed a scale for you to use when gauging your partner's performance and your levels of satisfaction. When your partner's performance falls within the ranges described below, consider the "satisfaction" explanation for each. This scale is based on my 33 years of practice working with clients' relationship problems.

> **0 to 40%** - Performance scores within this range tend to generate low levels of satisfaction. Relationships with scores within this range, especially if it involves

large numbers of expectations, are in very real danger of ending. Therapy or counseling should be considered to resolve problematic issues.

41 to 60% - Performance scores within this range indicate borderline levels of satisfaction. Relationships with scores within this range probably experience quite a few "ups and downs". Sometimes you're satisfied and sometimes you're not. If this situation persists and you're not able to change things using this guide, it may be to your advantage to seek professional help.

61 to 80% - Performance scores within this range indicate above average satisfaction levels. Relationships with scores within this range indicate there may be a few issues to resolve, but overall the relationship is in fairly good shape. Working toward improvements is desirable and will yield even higher levels of satisfaction.

81 to 100% - Performance scores within this range indicate high levels of satisfaction. There may be a few areas to monitor periodically, but probably little need for negotiations.

Exercise: Including Your Partner's Performance Scores

Take your list of expectations, the definitions, the importance score for each, the minimum level of acceptable performance (MALP) score, and include your partner's performance score on your index card. Remember that the score you assign is your careful estimate of your partner's behavior based on experiences you have had up to this point. As you recall your partner's performance in the last six months, be fair and realistic in your assessment. No matter how much objective data you have assembled, this will always be a subjective rating. You'll get close to "reality" but never be so accurate that your score is perfect. Remember, we are flawed human beings. We are not perfect and we don't have perfect recall of the past, no matter how hard we try.

DETERMINING AND SETTING PRIORITIES

This is a simple procedure requiring you to sort your expectations by the importance you gave to them and your partner's performance on each. This will help you to determine the order for presenting your expectations to your partner. Important relationship satisfaction issues will be at the top of your list and less important issues at the bottom. If you are using index cards, sort through your "deck" of cards to rearrange your expectations according to the directions below.

Exercise

First, make a list of your expectations. Next to each expectation place the importance score you assigned to it.

Second, add your MALP score (minimal acceptable level of performance) followed by your partner's performance score. Do this for each expectation. Your list should look something like the following:

	Importance	MALP	Partner's Performance
Expectation #1	7	50	65
Expectation #2	5	75	85
Expectation #3	8	75	50
Expectation #4	9	85	95
Expectation #5	3	50	35
Expectation #6	8	65	20
Expectation #7	3	50	95
Expectation #8	7	75	60
Expectation #9	7	65	85
Expectation #10	2	40	60

Third, rearrange your expectation list according to the importance score you assigned to each. Place the most important expectation at the top of the list. Continue to add expectations to your list <u>in their order of importance</u>. The least important expectation should be at the bottom of your list. Include the MALP score and your partner's performance score for each expectation. Your list should look something like the following:

	Importance	MALP	Partner's Performance
Expectation #4	**9**	85	95
Expectation #6	**8**	65	20
Expectation #3	**8**	75	50
Expectation #1	**7**	50	65
Expectation #8	**7**	75	60
Expectation #9	**7**	65	85
Expectation #2	**5**	75	85
Expectation #5	**3**	50	35
Expectation #7	**3**	50	95
Expectation #10	**2**	40	60

Fourth, review your expectation list starting at the top. As you scroll down the list (from top to bottom) select those expectations where **your partner's performance is below your MALP score**. Make a new list of those expectations **in the order selected**. Your list should look something like the following:

	Importance	**MALP**	**Partner's Performance**
Expectation #6	8	**65**	**20**
Expectation #3	8	**75**	**50**
Expectation #8	7	**75**	**60**
Expectation #5	3	**50**	**35**

You have now completed the priority setting procedure. In this example, four expectations have been identified and their order for discussion has been determined.

The remaining "non problematic" expectations may be explored in any order desired. Exploration of these expectations can further enhance the satisfaction levels already attained.

Now you are ready to negotiate with your partner on the items selected. It is assumed that your partner will have completed these same tasks with his/her set of expectations and be ready to sit down and work on them. On to Chapter 7.

NOTES

Chapter 7

NEGOTIATING AND COMING TO TERMS

NOTES

Chapter 7

NEGOTIATING AND COMING TO TERMS

Negotiating and coming to terms is difficult.

Presenting your ideas and listening to the ideas of your partner is complicated.

There are many pitfalls imbedded in the communication process.

Some of these problems have been discussed in previous chapters and are reviewed in later chapters. Don't hesitate to pause during the negotiating process if you are experiencing difficulties. Return to the previous chapters or look to Appendices A and B for assistance.

Participation in the negotiating process brings you into direct contact with your partner and potential conflict. It also brings with it many potential rewards, including love and happiness. Life presents many opportunities for success and gain, and, at the same time many opportunities for failure and loss. The "willingness to participate" in this process characterizes people who eventually get what they want.

The work you have completed thus far has been done primarily on an individual and private basis. Developing your list of expectations, defining each of them, determining their importance, and rating each are important tasks to do alone, without anyone else influencing your decisions.

Your partner, provided he/she has paralleled your work, will be sharing his/her ideas with you for the first time.

> Note: If you are presently without a partner, you may wish to stop at this point. However, read the remainder of the book and rehearse the process on your own if you would like. When a potential partner comes into your life, you will be ready for the negotiating process. You'll have only to share the book and encourage your

potential partner to complete the tasks already completed by you. What you have done thus far will allow you to logically and reasonably evaluate another person's ability to meet your expectations. Learning about and using these tools will give you a better chance for finding genuine love and happiness.

REVIEW

Before you actually begin the negotiating process, let's review some of the ground rules for good negotiation. Don't worry if you are finding it difficult remembering all of these communication ideas. If you get stuck, refer to this guide and then get back in the saddle. With practice and repetition your skills will improve and begin to feel like a natural part of your behavior.

Three-Step Process.

Good communication is a three-step process that helps insure accuracy and avoid misunderstanding.
      a. Active listening during the presentation;
      b. Feedback, or reflecting back what you heard;
      c. Confirmation that the feedback was accurate.

Backup and Discussion of Ideas.

Remember to discuss explanations of the ideas you present. Allow these explanations to be discussed rather than focusing on the main idea. You can come back to the main idea later. Your explanations form the backbone of your main idea, and can, through discussion, improve understanding.

Don't Assume.

When your partner communicates an idea, don't assume you know the meaning. Ask! It's the quickest way of finding out and making sure you are on target. Even if you are relatively sure, it can't hurt to get your assumption confirmed by asking.

Compromise.

Be prepared to compromise. It's okay to want your way and try to get it, but remember that your partner wants his/her way also! Don't hide what you want by playing games, be open and direct and risk not getting your way. Remember, compromise is really a sign of strength and rational thinking, not weakness. As you negotiate for your expectations, keep in mind that 100% satisfaction isn't an absolute requirement for a happy life. Realistic and practical thinkers settle for less than perfection.

Be Prepared for Conflicts.

Your partner's complexity and uniqueness will be increasingly revealed to you the more you get to know him/her. The chances for conflict will increase proportionately. This requires more patience, compromise, and problem-solving if you are to manage your relationship effectively.

Monitor Your Emotions.

Keep monitoring your emotions. Anger and irritation, anxiety and nervousness and guilt and shame are often signs of demanding or distorted thinking. Blaming yourself or others, dwelling on or anticipating the worst may seriously undermine the negotiating process. If this is occurring, stop and get your emotions under control, and then resume. Above all, don't put yourself down if you get upset! Guilt or depression about not keeping your emotions under control can be more detrimental than the original negative emotion itself.

After you and your partner have reviewed the above ground rules and have them well in mind, it's time to begin the negotiating process. Try to follow the suggestions given as closely as possible until you have had sufficient practice.

NEGOTIATION

Note: Before you actually begin, use the form found in Appendix D, the Negotiating Process Form. Make as many copies as you need and share them with your partner. Complete one of these forms for each expectation presented and use the forms for reference in your future meetings along with your index cards.

Step A. The first order of business is to decide *where* the process will take place. Make sure it allows for privacy and is free from interruptions. Pull the plug on the phone, or better yet, find a location away from home. If you are at home, you may want to meet when the children are asleep or when a baby-sitter is available to watch the children. The important thing is to provide a place for your negotiations that will allow at least one hour of uninterrupted time.

Step B. Next, take a look at your list of expectations. Before you pick an item to explore with your partner, make sure it is defined behaviorally. Remember, you want your definition to be specific enough so that it is observable and verifiable by observation. Your partner will know exactly what you are looking for and you will know exactly what to look for! Review the importance scores and reconfirm them to yourself. Do that with your partner's performance score as well.

Step C. After looking your definitions over, pick an item to present.

Step D. Now make a clear presentation of your idea. Use the three-step process (present the expectation, get feedback from your partner, give your partner confirmation about the feedback). Repeat your expectation as many times as necessary until your partner has an accurate understanding of it.

Step E. After completing Step D, ask your partner if it's okay to proceed. If there is any appreciable hesitancy, you may wish to choose another expectation and return to this one later. You don't want to present an expectation if your partner is not ready or willing to listen to it.

Step F. After agreement to proceed has been given, present your definitions. Your expectation will begin to take shape in your partner's mind as you define it. In addition, your partner will begin to develop behavioral objectives for him/herself. Let your partner know how important this expectation is to you. Remember to get feedback and give confirmation just as you did in Step D until you and your partner are certain that mutual understanding has been established.

Step G. Discuss any problems associated with the expectation. Let your partner know the changes you would like. Reveal your partner's "performance score" calculated previously. Give your partner an estimate of the performance score you would calculate if the above behavioral changes were made.

Step H. One hour is recommended for each negotiating session, thirty minutes for each partner.

1. After about 20 minutes, see if agreement can be reached concerning the issue.
2. Decide on behaviors necessary for change.
3. There may be substantial negotiating to do at this point. Your partner may not consider your expectation very realistic. Be prepared, if challenged, to examine your ideas for "reasonableness".
4. Keep revising the behavioral changes until BOTH of you are in agreement. The final agreement will probably be different from the version you originally intended.
5. Get a commitment from your partner to make the changes.
6. Set a time frame for these changes to occur. Usually it will be the next time you meet. You may want to monitor progress sooner than that. If that is the case, select the "checkpoints in time" and make note of them.

Step I. Once the negotiating is complete and the agreement is made, it's up to your partner to work on it. Keep in mind that it may not happen just the way you and your partner planned, even though you agreed. As a matter of fact, it may not happen at all! The results, good or bad, are to be monitored by you and any difficulty encountered discussed in your next session. Your job during this part of the process is to 1) monitor your partner's attempts, 2) rate his/her efforts, and 3) be prepared to present the performance rating in your next session.

__Important Note__: The continued inability to meet your expectations, provided there is the desire and the requisite knowledge and skills to do it, may be an indication of an "emotional" block. Getting to the bottom of this "emotional problem" has to do with keeping your emotions under control discussed in Chapter 3. Review Chapter 3 or go on to Appendices A or B, Troubleshooting the Process. If both these attempts fail, it may be time to consider contacting a professional for outside assistance.

Step J.   Now it is time for the complete process to be repeated with your partner presenting an expectation. Follow the same format as outlined above in Steps A - I.

Step K.   End the session. Before doing so, set another meeting time.

Step L.   Before your next session you and your partner have two jobs:

1.   Work to meet your partner's expectation; and,
2.   Monitor your partner's efforts at meeting your expectation.

It is suggested you keep good notes on your own successes and difficulties, with similar information concerning your observations of your partner's efforts. Logging such information will prove invaluable when you meet the next time. Get a pocket size Spiral notebook, carry it with you, and when appropriate, jot down your thoughts, concerns and ideas for later discussion.

Case Excerpt

You may find the following excerpt from a counseling session helpful in acquiring good negotiating skills. I will follow the above outline and identify the dialog in each segment. Note: this excerpt will show only one side of the two-sided expectation process.

Step A - Setting Up

In this instance, the session took place in my office, which automatically provided for privacy and an uninterrupted process.

Steps B & C - Reviewing Your Expectations for Clarity, Accuracy, and Importance

This client chose one of the more important expectations on her list, one that had been given an importance score of 7. She picked confidence and self-assurance and, as the expectation indicates, she expects her partner to be confident and self-assured. She gave the following definition:

"a person who asks my opinion, but does not rely on it in order to decide about things such as a job change or personal development and growth; a person who is able to disagree or be disagreed with without getting angry; a person who does not take it personally (feel I do not love him and mope about) when I choose to read alone or take a bath or go shopping by myself; and, a person who has his own interests and can pursue them with or without me."

After reviewing the definitions and the importance of the expectation and being satisfied with it all, the client was ready to go on to the next step.

Step D - Making a Clear Presentation

Jane: "I would like you to be confident and self-assured."

Bill: "One of the things that is important to you is to have a partner who is pretty sure of himself and rather confident in what he does. Is that correct?"

Jane: "Right! That is very important to me. I would give this an importance rating of 7."

Note: This couple got it on their first try; however, you may have to continue to repeat this step until both of you are sure of it. Remember the three-step process: *presentation, feedback, confirmation.*

Step E - Asking Your Partner if it's Okay to Proceed

Jane: "Is it okay with you if we talk about this expectation now?"

Bill: "Sure, why not!"

Step F - Defining Your Expectation

Jane: "Let me explain further what I mean by confidence and self-assurance. I would like my partner to ask my opinion about important matters, but not depend on me to make those decisions for him."

Bill: "You mean you would like me to come to you, get your input, but then go off and make my own decision?"

Jane: "Yes, that's right. But I only mean this for those decisions that basically affect you, and only have an indirect impact on me."

Bill: "Oh, I see. This would pertain to those things that are more personal for me. You wouldn't want me to do that if it affected you more directly, like selling the house or moving to another state?"

Jane: "Right. You've got it."

Bill: "So, if I am thinking about going to graduate school to further my career, you would want me to consult with you, but make the decision on my own."

Jane: "Yes, that's correct."

Bill: "Okay, what else?"

Jane: "I also want someone who isn't going to get angry when we have disagreements. This would also be a sign of confidence and self-assurance to me."

Bill: "I understand quite clearly. People who are intolerant of differences are likely to get irritated and angry when things don't go their way. Most of the time that's because they are so insecure that when differences emerge they get scared and threatened."

Jane: "Right! I want someone who is secure enough that we will be able to stand disagreements and be able to talk about them, not blow up over them."

Bill: "I think I know what you mean. What else?"

Jane: "Well, I also want someone who is self-assured enough not to whine and moan that I do not love him when I want to be alone. Privacy is important to me, and it has nothing to do with loving or not loving that person. Sometimes I like to read, or take a walk and think, just by myself."

Bill: "Yeah, me too! Time to be alone, just with yourself is also important to me, so you won't get any complaints from me on this point."

Jane: "The final important thing about having a confident partner is that he will have a variety of things that interests him, whether or not they interest me. And I would like him to pursue those interests actively."

Bill: "You mean you want someone who has a bunch of hobbies or sports interests that he would be vitally interested in. Would you want to be interested in those same things?"

Jane: "Not necessarily. If I am, that's okay, but a confident person will go ahead with them despite my interest. I am interested in doing some things together, but that's not what I am talking about here."

Bill: "I see. You want your partner to assert himself in what he likes, even if it isn't what you like."

Jane: "Right! And Bill, remember I have given this expectation a weight of 7, it's very important to me."

Note: This couple did exceptionally well in sending and receiving the definitions for this expectation; that's why I selected it for inclusion in this chapter. (Editorial changes have been made to more clearly convey the process.) You may not experience the same smoothness in your process, but I felt it was important for you to read a dialog that could be used as a "model". Keep going over the definitions, using the feedback-confirmation technique until all aspects of the definition are understood.

Step G - Discussing Problems Related to the Expectation

Bill: "Well, how well do you think I do?"

Jane: "Quite well, as a matter of fact. I would give you a 70 on this one!"

Bill: "A 70, I thought I was more confident than that! I would have given myself at least an 80, maybe even an 85!"

Jane: "Well, you do fine in just about all the ways I have indicated in my definition, but I think there is some room for improvement. If you did reach an 85, that certainly would be acceptable accomplishment as far as I am concerned."

Bill: "Okay. But just where do I need to improve?"

Note: There is a hint of defensiveness in Bill's response to Jane. He may be thinking she is being critical of him, rather than suggesting improvement of this particular trait. It is important for him not to take this personally, that is, seeing her evaluation as an indictment of him as a person. Rather, he could take this discussion with Jane and make some improvements in this area. If he sees it as "constructive criticism" and decides to make some changes, he is likely to get Jane to feel more satisfied and happy.

Jane: "Actually, there are two areas where I think you could improve. First of all, when we have had some disagreements in the past, you've gotten pretty angry on a few occasions, a few too many as far as I am concerned. I'm afraid if we continue, these outbursts will occur more frequently than they do now."

Bill: "When did I do that? I don't remember! And, what do you mean by getting 'pretty' angry?"

Jane: "A couple of months ago, we were watching that TV program on premenstrual syndrome? And they were saying that some women are so affected by it that they aren't responsible for what they do at those times of the month? Do you remember?"

Bill: "Yes, I remember!"

Jane: "And I said I agreed with them, that women so affected shouldn't be held responsible, since it was their biochemistry that was haywire! Then you really got angry. You started yelling, and walking around, and flailing your arms, and getting red-faced, I wasn't sure what you were going to do. You said that if you let someone off the hook, and blame biochemistry, that everyone would start doing that and claim immunity from their bad behavior. And then you started yelling about the insanity plea in criminal cases. I was scared to go on discussing the whole subject!"

Bill: "I guess I did get quite emotional."

Jane: "I would like it if you would let me get some of my ideas out before you start on a rampage. And, I would like it if you didn't go on a rampage like you did a couple of months ago. It's okay with me if you have strong feelings about something, and even express them, but don't get so angry. As a matter of fact, I started thinking about some of the points you made about that TV program, and have changed some of my ideas. I only wish we could have done that with less anger. After all, maybe it's natural to have disagreements like that, since we both don't think alike."

Bill: "I see what you mean; I'll work on controlling my anger more, especially when we disagree on something. Probably we'll have more of these disagreements the longer we know each other and explore more things together."

Jane: "Good. I'd really like that!"

Bill: "What's the other area I could improve in?"

Note: After getting through the process on this particular shortcoming, Bill now appears to be more willing to hear the next. This kind of enthusiastic anticipation is common once the process gets started. People begin to realize that it's **not so awful** to hear about their fallibilities. Sometimes when flaws are exposed, you don't have to spend so much energy trying to hide them. Bill can control his anger by realizing that the demanding thinking he is doing is the source of it. By changing his demanding thinking he can successfully lessen the degree of his emotional upset and be more accessible for rational discussion. Jane doesn't have to agree with him, and, although he would like her to think differently, that's under her control, not his! It's not awful if she doesn't agree with him! If he continues to encounter difficulty in controlling his anger, he might want to do some additional reading on the subject, or, if that doesn't work, seek professional assistance.

Jane: "It seems to me that most of the sports that interest you are those that require two people to play, and you expect me to play them with you. I would like it if you would either develop interests in 'singular' types of sports, like running or biking, or try to line up someone else to play with you from time to time. I don't always want to play tennis and backgammon when you do, but I feel if I don't you'll really be disappointed and pout for the evening!"

Bill: "You've always agreed to play when I've asked you. I thought you wanted to play and were interested in them as much as I was!"

Note: Jane has, through the presentation of this expectation, given Bill information that he never had. This frequently occurs although Jane may not have thought to do so consciously.

Jane: "I guess I should have been more honest with you, but I didn't want to disappoint you. Telling you things like this is one of the things I need to work on."

Bill: "I realize you aren't as interested in sports and games as I am. And I want you to know I wouldn't take it personally if you didn't want to do them. But let's talk about that in more detail when it comes time for me to tell you some of my expectations."

Bill: "About getting someone else to play or developing some interest in 'singular' sports, no problem, that will be easy. John and I were talking the other day and want to set up a time for some tennis. There isn't any reason we couldn't set something up on a regular basis. As far as the backgammon goes, I may have to look around and see if I can scare up some interest. Pete, at work, may be interested. I could always play on the Internet!"

Jane: "It's not that I wouldn't be interested in playing some of the time, I would, it's just that I would like you to have others you could play with. That would free me up."

Bill: "I understand. I'll work on that one. It may be more fun to have a variety of players, add spice to the game! If I made some of the changes we have just discussed, what kind of an improvement do you think I would get in my score?"

Jane: "I would be very happy with any effort you would make in this area, so you could easily get that 85 from me. Who knows, you might even get as high as a 95 if you did both of them.

Step H - Coming to Terms

Jane: "Well, I guess we've pretty well settled on this area. What do you think?"

Bill: "Yes, I think so. But let's review just what you're looking for and what I am going to do. You want someone who is confident and self-assured. You want someone who asks you for input, but makes decisions for himself. And you want someone who won't get angry when there is a disagreement. Stop me if I'm wrong."

Jane: "Keep going, so far, so good."

Bill: "You also want someone who will allow privacy without reading into it that he is not loved. And finally you want someone who has an interest in a variety of activities that he would be willing to do with himself or with someone other than you. Right?"

Jane: "Right!"

Bill: "And there are a couple of areas where I could make a number of changes that might help improve your satisfaction with my performance in this area. First, I could control my anger better, especially when we have a disagreement. Second, I could put forth more effort in getting others to play tennis or other activities with me instead of depending upon you entirely. And I do pretty well on the other two areas, privacy and decision-making. Right?"

Jane: "Right again! So you're going to work on that?"

Bill: "I'll give it a whirl. When are we going to get together for another session?"

Jane: "I was hoping we could meet again in two weeks."

Bill: "Okay, I'll try to have some results for you by then."

Jane: "Good! I'll be keeping my eye on you." (laughter)

Step I - Monitoring the Progress

Keep notes on successes, failures, and possible reasons for each during the period of time between the assignment and the next meeting. This step is not actually part of the immediate negotiating process, rather a step in the overall process.

Step J - Repeating the Process

Now repeat the entire process with your partner presenting his/her expectation to you following Steps A through I. When this has been completed, go on with Steps K and L.

Step K - Ending the Session

Jane: "So, we're going to meet in two weeks?"

Bill: "Sounds good to me. Same time, same station!"

Step L - Assignments
Remember to work on the ideas presented to you by your partner and monitor your partner's efforts at change.

I have included a form for this part of the process in Appendix D. Make copies of this form for yourself and your partner for each of the expectations you discuss.

Note: The particular expectation presented and the actual time taken responding to it will determine the time spent negotiating. If discussion of an expectation takes more than the 30 minutes per partner, by all means take the time. It is important to thoroughly explore each expectation that is presented. If your total time exceeds one hour and both of you agree to continue, then continue. Be aware of fatigue and end the session before it sets in. Negotiating when you are tired is not easy and often results in mistakes, intolerance and increased frustration. You can always meet again to pick up where you left off. In any case, alternate presenting expectations, first you, then your partner.

NOTES

Chapter 8

CONTINUING THE PROCESS:
REVIEW OF PREVIOUSLY
SELECTED EXPECTATIONS,
RECONTRACTING AND
SELECTION OF
ADDITIONAL EXPECTATIONS

NOTES

Chapter 8

—————⟫●⟨—————

CONTINUING THE PROCESS:
REVIEW OF PREVIOUSLY SELECTED EXPECTATIONS, RECONTRACTING AND SELECTION OF ADDITIONAL EXPECTATIONS

When the agreed amount of time has elapsed, meet again. You and your partner have had the opportunity to work on expectations previously discussed and monitor each other's efforts. If your discussion indicates the need for further work, recontracting to do that work will be necessary. In addition, you can select new items and continue the work described in Chapter 7. As you can well imagine, this effort is cumulative, making it necessary for each of you to keep track of the expectations discussed. Using the index cards and the Negotiating Process Form found in Appendix D in accordance with the instructions in Chapter 7 will make the process easier.

Before outlining the steps to be taken at this stage of the process, a review of the ground rules for good communication is in order. Remember to:

    a. Engage in active listening;

    b. Give feedback concerning what you heard;

    c. Give confirmation regarding the feedback received;

    d. Present explanations backing up your ideas;

    e. Ask for the meanings behind your partner's ideas;

    f. Be prepared to compromise;

    g. Approach the process with an acceptance and openness that is the hallmark of tolerance;

    h. Work hard and be willing to put in the effort in order to have a successful process; and,

    i. Monitor and control your negative emotions, especially your anger.

Step 1. Again, find a private place for your meeting to minimize interruptions. Get out your index cards and Negotiating Process Form and conduct a review to acquaint yourself with all of the information. Don't just review your monitoring notes, check the entire form and the cards.

Step 2. When you are ready to present and discuss the previously selected expectation, start with a statement of the expectation, the definitions of it, the importance score, the MALP score, and the performance score. Then go on to review your discussion notes, followed by the agreement the two of you reached (coming to terms). These reviews are very important in bringing the previous discussion to mind.

Step 3. Next present your observations of your partner's attempts at meeting your expectation using your monitoring notes. Rate your partner's performance for the period of time the change was attempted. After doing so, discussion can proceed with input from your partner concerning observations of the performance attempt and the ease or difficulty encountered. It is during this phase of the discussion where decisions can be made concerning further efforts to improve the score. The decision should be based on the level of satisfaction/dissatisfaction reached and the level of performance achieved. Consider the MALP score given this expectation earlier. If more work is indicated, decide what can be done, get a commitment to do it, and record the new agreement.

Step 4. Now your partner can repeat the same process reviewing the expectation presented to you. After this has been completed, you can go on with the selection of two new expectations following the directions found in Chapter 7. Remember to fill out a Negotiating Process Form for each expectation.

The dialog between Jane and Bill continues and illustrates this part of the process. Editorial changes have been made in the text to more clearly convey the process.

Step A - Setting Up

Again, Jane and Bill met in my office, insuring the uninterrupted discussion of their expectations.

113

CHAPTER 8 / Continuing the Process: Review of Previously Selected Expectations,
Recontracting and Selection of Additional Expectations

<u>Step B</u> - Reviewing Your Negotiating Process Form and Index Cards

Look over the entire form and the index cards. You may even want to make some additional notes about what you want to say or emphasize in the steps that follow. When you have given yourself adequate time to do so, go on to Step C.

<u>Step C</u> - Making a Clear Restatement of the Expectation, the Definitions, Importance Level, MALP Score, and Performance Rating

(Since your partner has previously agreed to consider this expectation, it is not necessary to get his/her go-ahead at this time.)

Jane: "The last time we met I presented my expectation concerning my desire for you to be confident and self- assured."

Bill: "Right!"

Jane: "Do you remember what I meant by that?"

Bill: "I think so, but why don't you go over that again?"

Jane: "Okay. What I said was that I want a partner who would ask my opinion about matters that involved him, but not depend on me for making the decision."

Bill: "Right, and there were three other elements. Why don't you just go on with them, we can talk about them after you have presented them."

Jane: "Okay. I also want someone who won't get angry when we have disagreements, someone who won't whine and moan when I want some time alone, and someone who will have a variety of interests to pursue himself whether they interest me or not."

Bill: "I remember all of those things, and I also remember the importance they had for you. You scored it a 7 as I recall, very important, and rated my performance around a 70. You also indicated a minimum acceptable performance level of 85 on this one."

Jane: "Right! You thought you did better than a 70, but after I presented some of my concerns you saw my point of view."

Bill: "Yes, I did, and after all, you have a right to see things from your point of view. Just because you rated my behavior a 70 doesn't mean that that is in fact a 70. Others may rate it differently, I may rate it differently. But, if I'm going to hang around with you, your point of view is going to be one of the most important ones for me to pay attention to."

Note: A behavior rating by your partner is a subjective opinion of your behavior based on your partner's observations. These observations are colored by the beliefs, philosophies, and ideas your partner has accumulated over the years of his/her life. In all probability your partner believes them to be true and accurate representations of how things are or should be. For this reason, consider your partner's opinions of your behavior to be important, but not necessarily how others or yourself would see the same behavior.

Step D - Review of Your Previous Discussion

Jane: "Do you remember all the details of our discussion the last time we met?"

Bill: "I think so. Let me try to outline it and you can correct me if I'm wrong."

Jane: "Fine."

sBill: "You are really interested in having a partner who is basically independent and very secure with himself, and who acts that way. Decisions, with some input from you, should be mainly the responsibility of the person it affects most. You want to give your point of view, but not make the actual decision. You also want someone who will give you privacy when you want it. Personal space is important to you and you want your partner to regard it as such. We both felt okay about these two areas, since neither of us anticipated

115

CHAPTER 8 / Continuing the Process: Review of Previously Selected Expectations,
Recontracting and Selection of Additional Expectations

any difficulty in meeting these expectations."

Jane: "Right."

Bill: "However, there were two areas where some work on my part was needed. You felt I needed to control my anger better especially when we disagreed, and to develop more varied interest in outside activities that didn't require your participation."

Jane: "And I gave you some examples."

Bill: "Sure. That helped and made it very clear to me what you wanted. Going over the argument we had over premenstrual stress and responsible behavior really helped pinpoint my angry behavior and illustrate to me what you didn't want."

Jane: "You knew exactly what I was talking about when it came to you having more varied interests and a variety of other people to do them with, thereby allowing me some freedom from being responsible for being the only person to do them with you."

Bill: "Well, how do you think I've done in the past two weeks?"

Note: Bill has just initiated the next phase of the process, observation of the partner's efforts.

Step E - Observations of Your Partner's Efforts

Jane: "Are you ready for this!"

Bill: "Lay it on me."

Jane: "First the anger. You controlled it, especially when Sally started talking about politics. And again, when she said 'men were short-sighted when it came to women's roles in government', and I agreed with her. I was pretty sure that had we not talked two weeks ago, and you hadn't been working on this, that you would have eventually blown up. Right?"

Bill: "Well, I did have to hold myself back a couple of times. It was hard, but I decided to put the brakes on."

Jane: "How did you manage to do it so well?"

Bill: "I told myself that you all had the right to your opinions, and that you didn't have to agree with me for me to hold on to my own opinions. I can live with my ideas and I don't have to have everyone agree with me for me to think my ideas are okay."

Jane: "Keep up the good work. I appreciate your efforts here. It'll make a big difference if we can live with each other, even though we have some different ideas on things. I don't think you could have done any better as far as I am concerned. I gave you a 100% for your effort over the past two weeks."

Bill: "Great! It's nice to know you noticed, and it felt good to me not to get so angry at differences of opinions. It really wasn't as hard as I thought it would be. 'Mind over emotions', you know!"

Jane: "I'd like to go on to the other area, the one of developing varied interests and of finding others to do things with. I didn't see much effort on your part here. What happened?"

Bill: "That's because most of what I've done to get others to do things with me has occurred at work. I've asked a few people if they were interested, but nothing has been set up yet. As far as doing some of the things on my own, I haven't felt well a good part of the past two weeks, you know, with my cold and my left shoulder. So I haven't felt like doing much of anything at all. You know I haven't asked you to do them with me. Right?"

Jane: "That's true. So based on what you are telling me, we'll have to wait a little longer to see the results for this particular item."

Bill: "Actually, not too much longer. Bob and I are playing racquetball next

117

CHAPTER 8 / Continuing the Process: Review of Previously Selected Expectations,
Recontracting and Selection of Additional Expectations

Wednesday evening, then you can watch TV to your heart's content."

Jane: "That will be nice. You used to want me to do that with you and I always resented missing my shows. Since not much has happened with this part of the expectation, my score on your performance is pretty much the same, but with the effort you put into controlling your anger, your overall score is up to at least an 80. At least in my opinion. What do you think?"

Bill: "I agree. Any problems with the other two aspects of your wanting a partner who is confident and self-assured? You know, asking for input regarding decisions and allowing you privacy without whining about it?"

Jane: "No, those weren't problems before and they still are fine with me."

Step F - Recommitment to Work on the Expectation

Bill: "Well, I'll keep working on the anger response much the same as I did during the last two weeks. This is an area that I had better keep working at if I'm going to teach myself a new way of responding. I did it, but it was hard, and I could see how I could easily slip back into my old ways. As far as doing things with others, I feel confident about this area and you'll see some evidence of effort soon."

Jane: "Sounds good to me. This is neat. I feel like we are really working in the right direction. I really feel happy about doing this."

Bill: "Me too!"

Step G - Review of Your Partner's Expectation of You

Follow Steps A through F.

Step H - Selecting Additional Expectations for Work

Follow Steps A through L in Chapter 7. As you can clearly see, this process can continue in a repetitive fashion for as long as it may take to cover the expectations you have selected.

Because of the cumulative nature of the process, it is extremely critical that notes be kept and the Negotiating Form be used as you continue. It is easy to forget, lose your place, or make errors. Remember, we're not perfect. We can use all the help we can muster when it comes to managing a relationship.

FINAL CONTRACTING AND PERIODIC REVIEW

You and your partner have now completed the expectation process. The only thing left to do, besides continuing to work at your relationship (remember, that really never ends), is to agree to meet periodically to review that "never-ending work". It can be every few months, or 6 months, or on a yearly basis. You can decide on any interval of time that is comfortable and convenient for you, but I recommend that it not be more than a year.

AT THIS POINT...

Congratulations on choosing to work on your relationship and for all your effort completing the tasks described in this book! You and your partner have learned the importance of meeting each other's expectations as a way of achieving love and happiness in your relationship. I can't guarantee you and your partner will always get the love and happiness you want, but I do believe each of you are now better prepared for it.

I confess that my approach for managing a relationship is far from romantic. However, I believe if you and your partner regularly use the principles described in this book, you will improve the chances for a more successful loving relationhip. Remember, work is required to get love and work will be required to keep it!

APPENDICES

NOTES

Appendix A

—————◦∈————

WHAT IF SOMETHING GOES WRONG! TROUBLESHOOTING THE PROCESS - PART I

LOW FRUSTRATION TOLERANCE, EMOTIONAL INTERFERENCE, AND COGNITIVE DISTORTIONS

"Murphy's Law" states that if something can go wrong, it will. I don't subscribe to rules predicting absolute certainty, but I can testify to the fact that I have never been part of an expectation negotiating process where everything went RIGHT! Anticipating a non-perfect process, where things can and do go wrong, makes sense. Being prepared for them is equally sensible. This appendix is designed to provide you with information and assistance for the "trouble" you may encounter in negotiating your expectations.

LOW FRUSTRATION TOLERANCE - LFT

When the expectation-sharing process breaks down, you can be relatively sure that Low Frustration Tolerance has played a prominent role. LFT is created by the view that **"things should not be as hard as they are"**. As a result of this idea, millions of people find themselves without energy, motivation, or even concern to do much about the problems that confront them. LFT prevents people from doing the work required to reach their goals. *One of the basic assumptions of this book is that hard work is necessary for love to be created and shared, and without hard work, you probably will not get the love you want. If you want to use this book, you will have to rid yourself of LFT.*

If you are among those with LFT, or if you have encountered some evidence of LFT in your partner, here are some ways of getting rid of it.

> *Note:* If you just completed reading the preface and decided to skip to this section of the book to work on LFT before starting the expectation process, it's good to have

you. If you completed the process, following the step-by-step instructions in the previous chapters, you probably don't have LFT. Instead, you are likely to have HFT (High Frustration Tolerance). HFT allowed you to complete all that work! Despite your HFT, I would recommend you keep reading. *You don't have to be sick to get better.*

A. Change Your Point of View.

Get rid of the idea that "things" shouldn't be as hard as they are!

Change such ideas as:
"This is too much for me to handle!", or
"Why me, it isn't fair that I have to do so much, others don't!", or
"I can't stand this, why is it so hard?", or
"Life should give me the things that I want, now!"

Adopt ideas like:
"I would prefer things to be easier for me to handle but it isn't, too bad!", or
"It would have been nice if I hadn't had to put in so much effort, but I did! Life isn't always fair that way!", or
"I can stand it but I don't like it that it is so hard!", or
"Where is it written that it shouldn't be so hard!", or
"Why should life give me the things that I want, even though it would be nice? I'd like to win the lotto, so does that mean that I should win?"

Changing your point of view to get rid of LFT and replacing it with HFT (High Frustration Tolerance) is strongly recommended. Life and living life is difficult for all of us. My clients, when asked about the ease and difficulty of living life, have all responded similarly. **"It is difficult!"** However, many of those who answer go on to add, **"But it shouldn't be so hard!"** These individuals have LFT and usually experience a great deal of frustration when faced with difficulty. But if life is hard, then why keep saying that it shouldn't be? If something is, then something is! Many people refuse to face this reality. Recognizing and accepting this basic fact is a healthy thing to do, and will be healthy for your relationship. It will also help you to get through this book. *It is better to face the reality that having a loving relationship is difficult and requires hard work!*

123

APPENDIX A / What If Something Goes Wrong! Troubleshooting the Process - Part I
Low Frustration Tolerance, Emotional Interference, and Cognitive Distortions

Problem: It also takes hard work to get rid of LFT, **repetitive hard work**. This poses a rather interesting problem. How do you get started doing something hard when you are thinking "this is too hard!"? The answer is simple - **you force yourself!** You force yourself to think differently as previously illustrated and you force yourself to act differently as illustrated below. You keep doing this over and over, until doing hard things isn't as difficult. So, by and large, you "condition" yourself to hard things by forcing yourself to do those things. It is somewhat of a paradox: *the more you do something that is hard, the easier it gets!* You can see this principle at work when you watch athletes engaged in conditioning exercises. To successfully condition themselves, weight lifters, runners and swimmers alike practice, practice, practice. They not only do this repetitively, they do it with the hardest exercises. *It takes precisely the same forced repetitive effort for you to be successful in tackling any difficult task that faces you, including the work in this book.*

Example: A person wants to run 2 miles as part of an exercise program for weight loss.

LFT Thoughts
"It really is TOO hot and
I'm really TOO tired!"

HFT Thoughts
"Even though it is hot, and I'm tired, running
will help me reach my goal of weight loss. I
can do it, although it will be hard!"

Exercise 1. LFT

In order to further clarify the differences between LFT and HFT, simply list currently held LFT thoughts that prevent you from completing a particular task. Then list the HFT thoughts that would allow you to complete the task next to each LFT thought. *Remember HFT thoughts are anti-LFT thoughts.*

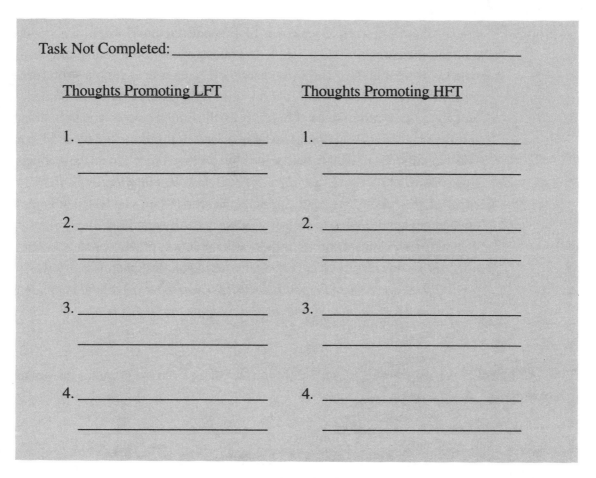

Task Not Completed: _____

Thoughts Promoting LFT   Thoughts Promoting HFT

1. _____   1. _____
   _____   _____

2. _____   2. _____
   _____   _____

3. _____   3. _____
   _____   _____

4. _____   4. _____
   _____   _____

B. Change Your Behavior.

Here are some things you can **DO** in order to get HFT.

Exercise 2. LFT

Without hesitation, put this book down and do something that you have been putting off for some time. Do it now. Don't think about it, just do it, and then come back to the book. Go and do it NOW!!

Now that you have done what you have put off, how do you feel? Was it as hard to do as you thought it would be? Did you get more enjoyment out of doing it than you thought you would?

125

APPENDIX A / What If Something Goes Wrong! Troubleshooting the Process - Part I
Low Frustration Tolerance, Emotional Interference, and Cognitive Distortions

If your answers surprise you, you have learned something very important!
Things may not be as difficult as you think. The enjoyment you get out of doing things, even hard things, may be greater than you thought.

Exercise 3. LFT

Arrange to be involved in an event where you are sure things will not go your way. In other words, plan to have something go just the opposite of what you would like. Have a failed outcome. This may sound like a strange request, but it really makes sense. Here's why: LFT is strongest when things don't go the way you think they should. Facing those things will allow you to practice thinking differently about them.

Try frying an egg without butter and try to keep from breaking the yolk when you turn it over. Or try lighting a fire in your fireplace with wet wood. Sunbathe on the beach and try to keep sand off yourself. Be creative, think of situations where there is little likelihood of things going your way. Do one of those things now and come back to the book after experiencing the negative outcome.

Now that you have experienced things not going your way, how do you feel? Was it hard for you to face things not going your way? Did you survive things not going your way? Could you accept the outcome?

It would be great if these two exercises could "cure" LFT. Unfortunately they can't. What they can do is get you started working on your LFT. When you experience LFT, stop, think about it, challenge your thoughts and force your behavior to be different. _Doing it makes all the difference._

EMOTIONAL INTERFERENCE

This is such an important troubleshooting topic, Chapter 3 is completely devoted to it. Since 99.9% of the readers of this book, as well as 99.9% of humanity will have difficulty with their emotions, this section is included here despite having an entire chapter devoted to it. This section has been arranged by type of emotion experienced. Each section will contain cognitive and behavioral methods for overcoming the problems encountered.

ANGER

Irritation and annoyance, even when felt strongly, usually occur when something happens that you wish hadn't. Such an undesirable occurrence is a nuisance and may impede progress toward your goals. You could have lived without such interference and would have preferred to do so. Your experience will be one of irritation, displeasure, and frustration.

Anger, when felt even mildly, also indicates a frustrating situation has occurred. But, in addition to your <u>preference</u> that it not occur, you <u>demand</u> that it not occur. This kind of thinking is illogical because it is contrary to the reality of the occurrence. When something occurs, it occurs. If something happens, it happens. It may not necessarily be good or desirable, but nonetheless, it occurred. No amount of thinking will change the fact that it occurred.

There are two rules to follow when you experience anger:

1. If you are <u>appropriately irritated and annoyed</u>, let yourself know and accept it, and, if you wish, express it to others; and,
2. If you are <u>inappropriately angry</u>, change it to appropriate irritation or annoyance, then express it to others.

In order to tell whether you are experiencing appropriate (rational) or inappropriate (irrational) anger or any emotion, check the *cognitive origins of the feeling*. In other words, go back to your thinking and identify the thinking style. *Is it preferential or demanding?*

<u>Preferential thinking will give you appropriate irritation</u>.
<u>Demanding thinking will give you inappropriate anger</u>.

Remember, thinking is comprised of ideas expressed through language. Ideas are comprised of word groupings that have certain meanings. Therefore, it is possible to determine whether thoughts are preferential or demanding by looking carefully at the words used.

127

APPENDIX A / What If Something Goes Wrong! Troubleshooting the Process - Part I
Low Frustration Tolerance, Emotional Interference, and Cognitive Distortions

<u>Preferential Words</u>	<u>Demanding Words</u>
wish	must
like	have to
desire	got to
want	should
hope for	

So, finding any of these words among the sentences running through your mind will help to determine the preferential or demanding nature of your thinking.

Exercise 4. Anger

Listen to others speak. Look for the "musts" and "shoulds" compared to the "likes" and "wants". Keep track of them and write them down. Try getting used to listening for them.

Exercise 5. Anger

After you have trained yourself to listen for these words, try to link the words to the "mood" and "behavior" of the person using them. Go on to the next paragraph ONLY after you complete this part of the exercise.

Example:
Words: "He must not be late." Mood and Behavior: Anger and hostility

<u>WORDS</u>	<u>MOOD & BEHAVIOR</u>
_____	_____
_____	_____
_____	_____
_____	_____

If you found the "musts" and "shoulds" linked to stronger emotions than "likes" and "wants", you have just demonstrated how *moderate thinking* leads to *moderate emotions* and how *stronger thinking* leads to *stronger emotions*.

Anger is intensified by adding thoughts of ***awfulization, intolerance*** *and* ***condemnation***.

➔ *Awfulizing* results in your making things worse than they are.

➔ *Intolerant thinking* teaches you that you can't stand things, people, or situations as they are.

➔ *Condemnation* results in your discrediting others for their wrongdoings or failure to please you.

All together, you can make yourself miserable - **miserably mad!**

Chapter 3 fully describes the irrationality of these three additional forms of thinking, so only limited explanation is given here. My primary goal is to help you give up ***awfulization, intolerance*** *and* ***condemnation***. Doing so will help you change your inappropriate anger to appropriate irritation.

AWFULIZING

A. Change Your Point of View

Strip your thinking of the idea that "It's awful, horrible, and terrible". Instead, start flooding your mind with the idea that "It's unfortunate, bad or undesirable".

Exercise 6. Awfulizing

Focus on something that you now believe to be awful, horrible, and terrible. Tell yourself that it is only unfortunate and undesirable. Do this ten times a day for the next week. At the end of the week compare your emotional reactions to those of the past. The difference you note will be due to what you

129

APPENDIX A / What If Something Goes Wrong! Troubleshooting the Process - Part I
Low Frustration Tolerance, Emotional Interference, and Cognitive Distortions

have told yourself. "You see, it's not the things of life that disturb us, but our view of them." (Epictetus, 1st Century, A.D.)

B. Change Your Behavior

Exercise 7. Awfulizing

Identify something that you consider awful, like a funeral or a cemetery, or being caught in a rainstorm without an umbrella. Write down all the characteristics that make the situation awful. Then place yourself in that situation. After doing so, force yourself to find things about the situation that are opposite characteristics of awful. Write these characteristics next to those previously written.

Describe the situation:

_____

_____

_____

Things that are awful:

_____

_____

_____

_____

Things that are non-awful:

_____

_____

_____

_____

The fact that situations have redeeming qualities proves the awfulization view to be inaccurate. By definintion, anything that is awful could not have a single redeeming quality. Try to expand this new awareness by repeating this exercise in a number of situations previously defined by you as awful.

INTOLERANCE

Intolerance is the third style of thinking that plays a significant role in the creation of anger. Believing that you "can't stand it", whatever it is, is a common misconception that is popular among humans. It is an inaccurate way of saying that you don't like something. Instead of thinking "I don't like it", you think "I can't stand it". This is a distortion that commonly occurs.

Fact: There is only one thing you will not be able to stand in your lifetime: the thing that finally does you in, the thing that leads to your demise. That only happens once, and obviously it hasn't happened yet. You have successfully, although not always easily, stood everything that has occurred in your life. If you hadn't, you wouldn't be alive. In all probability you will live until your mid-seventies or beyond and stand each and every thing that happens to you until that fateful day. Consequently, it doesn't make sense to tell yourself you can't stand something when you can and will.

A. Change Your Point of View

Exercise 8. Intolerance

Repeat after me! "I can stand it, but I don't like it!" Again, "I can stand it, but I don't like it!" Keep repeating this phrase over and over again, twenty or thirty times a day! By doing so you will begin to convince yourself that things are tolerable, but not necessarily likable or desirable.

B. Change Your Behavior

Exercise 9. Intolerance

Now place yourself in a situation previously thought to be intolerable.

Note: Do not include any situation that is physically dangerous or life-threatening, illegal, or places your job or any other important aspect of your life in jeopardy.

131

APPENDIX A / What If Something Goes Wrong! Troubleshooting the Process - Part I
Low Frustration Tolerance, Emotional Interference, and Cognitive Distortions

Make it something similar to the situation described in Exercise 7, or the situation you chose for that Exercise. Observe your reaction. Was it the same as previously experienced, before you told yourself you could stand it but didn't like it? Expand this exercise by continuing to experiment with things previously thought not bearable.

CONDEMNATION

Condemnation is the third cognitive element to consider in the problem of anger. Condemning others for failure to please you completes the anger reaction and may frequently result in extreme, violent, destructive behavior. Condemnation assigns worthlessness to a person or situation. If something or someone is worthless, then it is well to be rid of it or him/her.

A. Change Your Point of View

Exercise 10. Condemnation

Repeat after me - "Just because something (someone) doesn't please me doesn't make it (him, her) worthless. Just because I can't have my way and it (he, she) isn't giving me my way doesn't mean it (he, she) deserves damnation. I am not the ultimate judge of the world, and therefore I do not possess the power to damn it (anyone)." Repeat, repeat, repeat those sentences! Repeat them until you have convinced yourself they are true. Statements that accurately reflect reality are more likely to be truthful statements. And there is nothing more real than admitting our powerlessness to control the world and the people in it.

B. Change Your Behavior

Exercise 11. Condemnation

Pick an activity where you typically have a very good chance of things not going your way. Trying to pick up a small object while wearing heavy gloves or light a fire in your fireplace using wet wood. Keep trying to be successful, even though you are certain not to succeed. Then "damn" the gloves, the object, the wood, yourself, and anything else that keeps you from getting what you want. Lay it on thick, I mean really thick. Exaggerate the damnation about your incompetence until it becomes very clear to you how foolish your thinking is.

Change your thinking as outlined in Exercise 10. Then, take the object, the gloves, the wood, and yourself and write down all the positive characteristics of each. It should be clear that the negative characteristics assigned to these things and yourself were largely due to not getting your way rather than their innate value.

I have devoted a lot of this chapter to anger and the kinds of thinking that promote it. Anger seems to be the most destructive emotion interfering with the problem-solving process. A more trouble-free process between you and your partner is likely when anger is kept under control.

ANXIETY

Anxiety plays a significant role in the expectation process. It interferes by holding people back from taking risks. It creates avoidance behavior.

If you keep an idea, a feeling, or a behavior to yourself rather than sharing it with your partner, you deny your partner very important information. Most people do this out of fear. They fear their ideas, feelings, or behaviors if exposed, will pose danger to themselves in some way.

This kind of thinking does not make sense. First, since living life on planet Earth is inherently full of dangers, both perceived and real, avoiding them is impossible. Real dangers exist, and since they <u>do</u> exist, they <u>should</u> exist. To think otherwise - that they should not exist - is what I call "crooked thinking". For most of life's real dangers, taking reasonable precautions can effectively reduce risks. Second, most of life's anxiety reactions are caused by perceived dangers rather than real dangers. They only <u>feel</u> like they are dangerous. Much of the anxiety experienced by people is largely unnecessary and interferes with taking risks.

133

APPENDIX A / What If Something Goes Wrong! Troubleshooting the Process - Part I
Low Frustration Tolerance, Emotional Interference, and Cognitive Distortions

Anxiety can be understood in yet another way. When you think of something in the future and consider it dangerous, you will feel anxiety. *If you add the idea that you must protect yourself from that danger, and, in addition, believe you will not be successful, you will feel high levels of anxiety, maybe even panic.*

There is a style of thinking that will almost always ensure excessive anxiety. I call this possibility thinking. I'm talking about identifying one possibility, dwelling on it in a negative or catastrophic way and generating large quantities of anxiety. Let's try it!

Exercise 12. Make Yourself Anxious

Place yourself in a safe position but in a place where something can happen. For example, stand under a tree, look up at the branches above you, and begin to imagine the possibility that one of the branches is about to fall on you. In addition, imagine that you will be crushed and will live the rest of your life paralyzed. Think these ideas over and over again. Observe how you are feeling. Are you feeling more nervous, more apprehensive? If not, keep thinking this way until you do; then go on to the next paragraph.

Now, without moving from under the tree, begin to think differently. Start thinking that although a branch might fall on you and lead to paralysis, the likelihood of that happening is quite remote, and even if it did, it would be quite unlikely to cause paralysis. After all, the tree has existed for many years without dropping any of its branches, so the chance of that happening right at this precise moment is very unlikely. Now what kinds of feelings are you experiencing? Did your apprehensive and nervous feelings diminish?

In addition to possibility thinking, anxiety can be created by a number of other styles of thinking.

1. Discomfort Anxiety

This form of anxiety results from Low Frustration Tolerance (LFT). The term, discomfort anxiety, coined by Albert Ellis, describes the emotional state of a person who experiences anxiety when feeling or anticipating discomfort. It is based on the belief that discomfort should not exist, is awful, and should be avoided at all costs. Any action taken to avoid discomfort is legitimized. Fear increases when one thinks about the possibility of <u>not avoiding</u> discomfort.

When change is suggested during the *expectation process*, partners may anticipate discomfort making the change. As their anxiety increases, avoidance behaviors may increase as well, placing the expectation process in jeopardy. <u>Facing</u> discomfort and <u>accepting</u> it as a condition of life, and as a condition inherent in the expectation process, remains the best way to overcome discomfort anxiety.

A. Change Your Point of View

Exercise 13. Discomfort Anxiety

Instead of sticking to the idea that discomfort is awful and should not exist, start telling yourself that discomfort is part of life, and even though it is unpleasant, it is not awful. It might go something like this: "It's certainly not fun to feel bad (uncomfortable), but such is life. It would be nice if I could feel better, but at this time it doesn't seem likely that I will. It is impossible to feel good all the time. I've felt bad before and I've stood it, so I'll be able to stand it again! It's not 'dangerous' to feel bad, only uncomfortable".

B. Change Your Behavior

Exercise 14. Discomfort Anxiety

Now put yourself in a situation where it is likely that you will feel bad. For example, if you "hate" paying bills, pay some bills. If the cold makes you uncomfortable, go out in the cold, or if heat feels bad, leave the comfort of your air conditioned car, home, or office. When you are in the uncomfortable situation, start telling yourself how awful it is, how you can't stand it, how dangerous it is, and how it is going to do you in.

After you get yourself upset, change your thinking to those noted in Exercise 13. After doing so, note the difference in your level of anxiety. Does it seem less intense after talking yourself "down"?

135

APPENDIX A / What If Something Goes Wrong! Troubleshooting the Process - Part I
Low Frustration Tolerance, Emotional Interference, and Cognitive Distortions

2. Symptom Stress

This emotional state is characterized by increasing levels of anxiety. The more anxiety you feel the more fearful you become about the feelings you are having or anticipate having. People sometimes worry about getting emotionally upset, and when they do, they get more upset. Since this is uncomfortable, some people try to avoid getting upset in the first place. This may be accomplished by avoiding all those things that are potentially upsetting, including the change process suggested in this book. In extreme cases, it may take the form of "agoraphobia", a condition where a person refuses to leave their home. Staying at home is their way of avoiding triggers that may result in emotional upset which is viewed by them as intolerable and awful.

A. Change Your Point of View

Exercise 15. Symptom Stress

Issue more factual statements to yourself! Start telling yourself the truth! Instead of telling yourself that you shouldn't feel the way you do, start telling yourself that you would prefer to feel better. Instead of telling yourself that it is awful to feel bad and that you can't stand it, start telling yourself that it is only uncomfortable and unfortunate to feel bad, and that you can stand it. Instead of telling yourself that this feeling is going to do you in, start telling yourself that in all the years of feeling bad, it has never yet done you in and therefore, is unlikely to do so now. Keep telling yourself the truth, over and over again.

B. Change Your Behavior

Exercise 16. Symptom Stress

Put yourself in an "anxiety-provoking situation" previously experienced by you. Let yourself get anxious by giving yourself the "anxiety-provoking messages" noted above. When you have gotten yourself sufficiently anxious, change the messages to the "anxiety- reduction" ones noted above. Evaluate the change in your emotional state. If you are having difficulty doing this, write the two sets of messages side by side.

Anxiety-Provoking Messages	Anxiety-Reduction Messages
I shouldn't feel so bad, what's wrong with me?	Why shouldn't I feel bad from time to time!
I can't stand this feeling! This is awful!	I can stand this, although I don't like to feel this way!
If I don't calm myself down, I'm going to do myself in!	Getting upset isn't going to kill me!

When you put yourself in a situation and tell yourself these things, you accomplish two very important objectives. First, you give yourself the "opportunity" to challenge your disturbances. Second, you prove by actually doing it and surviving it, that your "fear" is exaggerated. Remember, when doing these "experiments", don't place yourself in any physical danger, do anything illegal, or jeopardize your job or other important aspects of your life.

3. Fear of Failure

This is simple. People think that to fail is the worst possible thing that could ever happen. The difficulty of the situation doesn't matter, our society expects and demands success. This generates anxiety in abundance. If you don't get over your fear of failure, you will not be willing to take risks. Unwillingness to take risks leads to failure by default. The cycle is completed by self-downing for failing. A very destructive cycle!

A. Change Your Point of View

Exercise 17. Fear of Failure

Tell yourself that "failing is part of life and characteristic of all humans". Tell yourself "failing is just as commonplace as the sun coming up each morning". Tell yourself "failure happens, it's not good, but nobody's perfect". Repeat these ideas to yourself over and over!

137

APPENDIX A / What If Something Goes Wrong! Troubleshooting the Process - Part I
Low Frustration Tolerance, Emotional Interference, and Cognitive Distortions

B. Change Your Behavior

Exercise 18. Fear of Failure

Again, this is simple. Do something. It doesn't matter what it is, or if you succeed or fail at it. When you have decided what you want to do, but before you succeed or fail at it, tell yourself that you can't fail. Tell yourself that it would be awful if you did and that everything would be lost if you failed. Let yourself "feel" the "fear of failure".

Now change your thoughts as you are about to embark on the task. Tell yourself that you hope not to fail, but if you do, it's bad, but not too bad. Tell yourself everyone fails from time to time, and that there's no reason for you to be the exception. Note the change in your feelings. Did the "fear of failure" go away or lessen? Now go on with your task. How did you do? Better than you expected? Reducing your fear of failure will improve your likelihood of success.

4. Defensiveness

When people are afraid, they tend to protect themselves. This is true psychologically as well as physically. There seems to be a tendency for us to act in ways to "preserve the integrity of the organism". By doing so, we survive. Psychological maneuvers are used to accomplish this. When we're maneuvering, we're not too interested in others but more in self-preservation.

A. Change Your Point of View.

Exercise 19. Defensiveness

To reduce defensiveness, tell yourself it is important to protect yourself against real danger but not very useful to protect yourself against perceived danger. Remind yourself that the perceived danger isn't as dangerous as you are making it. Ask yourself if you are going to really be done in by the thing you are facing. Ask yourself if the bad outcome were to occur, would you survive. Think about the worst case scenario, and ask yourself if that situation warrants holding back as much as you are.

B. Change Your Behavior

Exercise 20. Defensiveness

Put yourself in a situation where you have previously acted defensively. It might be where you don't know something but have maintained that you do, and won't admit that you don't know. Now, let your defenses down. Admit that you don't know it. After doing so, ask yourself if admitting this inadequacy was as bad as you had anticipated. Ask yourself whether the defenses were really necessary. Observe that you survived this admission of inadequacy.

SHAME, GUILT AND DEPRESSION

Shame, guilt, and depression can also play a significant role in interfering with the expectation process. They slow a person down, promote inactivity, create lack of motivation and generate disinterest. It is very important to rid yourself of these feelings if you are going to engage in a successful expectation process.

Shame, guilt, and depression have a common outcome: self- downing. Once a person has "downed" him/herself, the depressive response is completed with feelings of hopelessness and helplessness. These three outcomes, hopelessness, helplessness and self-downing are irrational for the following reasons:

> People are not helpless, they only think they are. If, for biological reasons, someone were not able to think or act, then we might declare that particular person helpless. The evolution and survival of humankind through eons of time are testimony to human ingenuity, adaptability and flexibility. Could helplessness yield such results?

> For the vast majority of people, there is hope. As long as we possess the ability to think and act and impact the next moment, there is hope. For as long as we live there will be a "next moment", so there is hope. There is only one moment when there is no hope, the last moment of our lives. And this one last moment, out of billions of moments that occur during our lifetime, occurs only once!

139

APPENDIX A / What If Something Goes Wrong! Troubleshooting the Process - Part I
Low Frustration Tolerance, Emotional Interference, and Cognitive Distortions

Depreciation of the "self" (self-downing) is equally illogical. It is impossible to globally evaluate a person. All events, decisions and behaviors of the person for all time would have to be available for review in order to conduct a complete evaluation. Even if all of those experiences (about 7.5 billion in an average lifetime) were available, what would the likelihood for those experiences to be all bad or all good? Not very likely! So, we end up with mixed results. Not very convincing data to make an overall global rating.

There are two types of guilt and shame. Appropriate guilt and shame and inappropriate guilt and shame. Appropriate guilt is created when we feel bad over our harmful behaviors. Appropriate shame is created when we feel bad about our behaviors when reminded of it by others. Inappropriate guilt is created when we down ourselves for our harmful behaviors. Inappropriate shame is created when we down ourselves about our behaviors when reminded of it by others. When behaviors are harmful to ourselves or others, then guilt and shame is appropriate. When appropriate, these feelings help keep us from engaging in harmful behaviors.

A. Change Your Point of View

Exercise 21. Inappropriate Guilt

Tell yourself you are a "louse" for not doing something that you should have. Let yourself feel "guilty". Then, start telling yourself that no matter what you did or didn't do, whether right or wrong, it will never turn you into a "louse". Write this idea down! Tell yourself that many people have differing ideas about what is "right and wrong" but the most important aspect of "right or wrong" behavior is whether it is harmful to yourself or others.

B. Change Your Behavior

Exercise 22. Inappropriate Guilt

Do something that for all or much of your life you have felt guilty, but that has not been harmful to yourself or others. Something like eating the last piece of candy or food that you know one of your kids wants, or not holding a door open for a "little old lady".

Now "blast" yourself for acting so badly, let yourself have it right between the eyes. Feel the guilt.

Now change your thinking. Tell yourself that it wasn't very nice not to help the "little old lady" but that it hardly makes you a "louse". Now how do you feel? You might still feel somewhat bad for not being very nice, but do you feel as guilty? Keep working it until you have reduced the guilty feeling to mild or moderate levels.

A. Change Your Point of View

Exercise 23. Inappropriate Shame

Repeat Exercise 21, but instead of telling yourself <u>you</u> should or shouldn't have done something, tell yourself you are a louse if <u>someone else</u> thinks you should or shouldn't have done something. Tell yourself that if <u>they</u> thought poorly of you, it would prove you to be a louse. Then, as in Exercise 21, change this thinking.

B. Change Your Behavior

Exercise 24. Inappropriate Shame

Put yourself in a situation where others are likely to rate you poorly for behavior they view as "bad". After feeling shameful, challenge and change this feeling to mild regret even through others are so disapproving. The situations can be the same or similar to the ones referred to in Exercise 22.

DEPRESSION

Hundreds of books and articles and research have been written and conducted on the subject of depression. It remains one of the most disabling emotional disturbances that exist. If extreme and severe, depression can lead to suicide. Therefore, depression should not be

141

APPENDIX A / What If Something Goes Wrong! Troubleshooting the Process - Part I
Low Frustration Tolerance, Emotional Interference, and Cognitive Distortions

taken lightly. David Burns has written an excellent book about depression and recently revised and updated it. It is entitled <u>Feeling Good: The New Mood Therapy</u> and I heartily recommend reading it, especially if you are having feelings of depression. If depression remains a problem, psychotherapy may be a good idea.

A. Change Your Point of View

Exercise 25. Depression

Recall the last time you were depressed or feeling "down". Do an ABC analysis of it.

A - The Situation/Event was _____

_____

_____

_____

_____

C - My Feelings and Behavior were _____

_____

_____

_____

_____

_____

B - Because I was Thinking (look for hopelessness, helplessness, and self-downing
     thoughts) _____

_____

_____

_____

D - I got out of my depression by Thinking_____

_____

_____

_____

_____

E - After I got myself undepressed I started Doing _____

_____

_____

_____

_____

The important thing to note here is the *change in thinking* followed by a *less depressed emotional state* and *increased activity*.

COGNITIVE DISTORTIONS

Thinking in *distorted* ways is almost certain to foul up the communicative process, just as LFT and emotional interferences do. If you or your partner think along the lines of any of the styles listed below, try to eliminate them. You may want to read Burns' book for more help.

EMOTIONAL REASONING

Problem: You "believe" your feelings, especially the negative ones. Because your feelings exist, you assume they reflect the truth. Therefore, you make decisions based on them.

Solution: Don't "believe" your feelings, especially the negative ones. First, check out the thinking that is behind them. After reflection, if you decide your feelings are appropriate, then go with them.

JUMPING TO CONCLUSIONS

Problem: You assume you are right and don't check things out. You predict future outcomes and are convinced predictions will be accurate. You then make decisions based on your predictions.

Solution: Don't assume your predictions are right. Let the facts of the situation determine the truth. Remember, you can't predict the future, you are not a "fortune teller" with a crystal ball.

143

APPENDIX A / What If Something Goes Wrong! Troubleshooting the Process - Part I
Low Frustration Tolerance, Emotional Interference, and Cognitive Distortions

PERSONALIZATION

Problem: You take personal responsibility for things that are happening around you that you are not responsible for, especially negative things. You blame yourself for these things happening.

Solution: Look at what is happening, determine your role using the facts available, and make yourself aware of your limitations. Remember, you are a person, not a magician with magical powers controlling the outcome of events.

SHOULD STATEMENTS

Problem: You demand things be the way you think they should. (I've spent a lot of time discussing this style of thinking, so I'll not do so here.)

Solution: Change your should thinking to a more preferential style, like "I wish" or "I would like".

MENTAL FILTER

Problem: You latch on to one single event, usually a negative one, and dwell on that exclusively.

Solution: Recognize that one event is <u>one</u> event, and deserves only the time and energy that one out of billions of events deserves.

DICHOTOMOUS THINKING

Problem: This is "black and white" thinking and very common. In this style of thinking, there are only two options. If it isn't one way, then it must be the other.

Solution: Admit that there are "shades of gray", even though life becomes more complicated when you look at things this way. When you find yourself in a problem situation, keep thinking about it until you have generated more than *two* alternative solutions.

OVERGENERALIZATION

Problem: You conclude from one single event that <u>everything</u> is just like it.

Solution: See one single event as one single event among many. Be a good scientist and look for data/facts that might disagree with any conclusions or overgeneralizations you might make.

DISQUALIFYING THE POSITIVE

Problem: You discredit positive events/data/facts in order to maintain your previously held ideas and beliefs.

Solution: Again, allow the data to determine your conclusions. Give up the idea that your previously held ideas and beliefs are correct.

MAGNIFICATION / MINIMIZATION

Problem: You exaggerate and make things more or less than they are. You "distort" the reality around you.

Solution: See things the way they are. Again, be a good scientist. Let the data/facts/ reality determine what is.

LABELING / MISLABELING

Problem: You label yourself or others, usually with a label that totally describes you or others (overgeneralization). As a result of this label you find yourself "stuck" with it and become a prisoner of the label despite contradictory evidence.

Solution: Stop labeling! Describe elements of a situation, or describe traits, character-istics, or behaviors of yourself or others. Do not try to describe the "global" picture.

145

APPENDIX A / What If Something Goes Wrong! Troubleshooting the Process - Part I
Low Frustration Tolerance, Emotional Interference, and Cognitive Distortions

NOTES

NOTES

Appendix B

WHAT IF SOMETHING GOES WRONG! TROUBLESHOOTING THE PROCESS - PART II

COMMUNICATION PROBLEMS, ROMANTIC BLOCKS AND LOW MOTIVATION

As you and your partner continue sharing expectations, other difficulties may disrupt the process. This appendix, like the preceding one, is designed to help you identify and eliminate blocks to progress.

COMMUNICATION PROBLEMS

A. Clarification

Failure to clarify the meaning of an idea is a common error frequently encountered in the communication process. The primary reason for such laxity is the belief that one's partner understands the other without having to provide a detailed explanation. Sound familiar? It should. It's the same old LFT problem discussed in the last chapter. Getting rid of LFT will help to improve the clarity of your statements. Go back to Appendix A, read about LFT, and then return to complete the following exercise.

Exercise 26.

Sit down with your partner for a discussion. Tape record the session so that you and your partner can listen to it after the discussion. Now present a vague idea so that there is little possibility of your partner understanding. Do that now!

Begin to clarify your communication gradually. After five minutes or so of increasing clarification, stop and listen to what you have recorded. Make note of your efforts. Discuss your partner's level of understanding at the beginning, middle, and end of the five minute session. Did your partner's understanding increase as clarification increased?

B. Feedback

The person to whom communications are being directed has the responsibility of decoding the message. Feedback behavior includes a.) active listening (really listening "hard"), b.) asking questions, and c.) telling the "communicator" what you heard. This process should continue until a clear meaning has been obtained.

Exercise 27.

Repeat Exercise 26, but this time have the "listener" do the clarifying following the steps noted above, listening, questioning, and giving feedback. Again, after 5 minutes or so, stop, and listen to the tape recording. Comment on your partner's effort to gain clarification from the message.

C. Not Enough Interaction

If the "clarification" and "feedback" steps are followed, a clearer and more accurate message will have been sent and received. When this doesn't occur it's usually due to insufficient effort. Again, LFT thinking will lead to a premature ending of the clarification/feedback exchange. Statements like "This shouldn't be taking so long!", or "We should have gotten it by now!" are common LFT thoughts that will stop the process before it is completed.

149

APPENDIX B / What If Something Goes Wrong! Troubleshooting the Process - Part II
Communication Problems, Romantic Blocks and Low Motivation

Exercise 28.

Combine Exercises 26 and 27, but this time do it for 10 minutes. Don't complain and say it's not necessary; that's your LFT talking. Just do it! Again, record the effort. Listen to it and note the increased clarity that results. After you have completed this exercise, ask if the effort required was as difficult as anticipated, or if the time required was too long.

D. Attribution and the Assumption Error

This is a common mistake where you attribute certain meaning to your partner's behavior without asking your partner about the meaning. You see the behavior, you evaluate and arrive at a conclusion about its meaning and you base your response on your conclusions. Obviously, this is ill-advised. What if your conclusion is inaccurate or downright wrong! It doesn't make sense to base your response on a "wrong" conclusion or a "false" premise.

Exercise 29.

Observe your partner doing something. Don't talk about it with him/her. Then write down all the possible meanings of the behavior. For example, your partner is sleeping. That can mean a number of things:

      a. your partner is tired;
      b. your partner is not interested in you;
      c. your partner is lazy;
      d. your partner is pretending to be tired;
      e. your partner's back must be hurting; or,
      f. your partner must not have gotten enough sleep last night.

After you have completed your list, ask your partner what the sleeping meant. You will learn many of the meanings listed were incorrect, and, if you had based your response on any one of them, you would have had a one in six chances of being correct, provided of course there weren't any additional meanings that you failed to include in your list.

ROMANTIC BLOCKS

Romantic notions (unrealistic love ideas) are detrimental to the health of relationships. This may sound like sacrilege, but it is true. The detrimental nature of such notions lies in their ability to distract one from the realities of the relationship and the work required to keep it functioning properly. Properly functioning relationships have a greater capacity for producing satisfaction. Therefore, eliminating romantic ideals will enable more progress to be made during the expectation process.

Note: All of the following ideals, when they are not met, tend to trigger feelings of depression, anger and anxiety.

Romantic Block #1. <u>My Partner must give love only to me.</u>

This romantic notion is based on the idea that there is a "one and only", and you should confine your love to that "one and only". If you love someone else, it definitely means you don't love your partner because you can't love two people at the same time. This idea extends to other individuals with whom you may have a positive, loving relationship, including parents, children, friends, and relatives. It doesn't matter, love shared with others is love denied to your "one and only". This may trigger a self-downing response in your partner. In addition, there may be a desperate attempt to get you to give your "one and only" the love that is required. It doesn't matter what you want.

Romantic Block #2. <u>My partner must give me love when I want (need) it.</u>

Delay is damaging. Delay is like a death sentence. Delay is intolerable. Because of the belief that "desired" love is **needed and absolutely required**, there can be no delay. And, somehow, you should be knowledgeable when this need strikes, so that you can administer life-sustaining love. Again, it doesn't matter what you want, it's what your partner **needs**. And, if you loved your partner, you would be unquestioningly and selflessly attempting to save your beloved partner's life.

151

APPENDIX B / What If Something Goes Wrong! Troubleshooting the Process - Part II
Communication Problems, Romantic Blocks and Low Motivation

Romantic Block #3. <u>My partner must guarantee me love.</u>

No ifs, ands, or buts here. There must be a guarantee or absolute assurance of love and, with it, a guarantee against uncertainty concerning its loss. Your failure to offer such assurance means you don't love your partner, never did, and never will. To be sure, you will fail, not only because the idea is impossible in the first place, but because of your fallible nature as a human. Anger, resentment, and anxiety are emotions frequently related to this romantic notion.

Romantic Block #4. <u>My partner must prove love and loyalty to me.</u>

Self-doubt and self-worthlessness lead people to believe in this romantic ideal. You are responsible to prove to your partner that he/she isn't as "bad" as he/she believes. You must convince your partner of his/her worth and lovability despite his/her belief to the contrary. If you fail to do so, it proves you don't care. If you don't care, it's because of your partner's worthlessness, and proves your partner unlovable.

Romantic Block #5. <u>I must feel very excited (emotional) when around my partner.</u>

"I should be happier than I have ever been!" Your partner reasons that strong, positive feelings are evidence of true love, and that without these feelings, it proves otherwise. Of course, the ups and downs of your emotional life separate from the relationship is not taken into account here. If your partner is around you and your partner doesn't feel excited, there must be something wrong. And the thing that is wrong is that your partner is not in love.

Romantic Block #6. <u>My partner should know what I want without me having to say.</u>

This idea is based on the "natural/spontaneous" myth. This myth postulates that natural or spontaneous action is better than planned or premeditated action. If you really love me, you shouldn't have to think about it. It will "just" occur. This ideal minimizes the learning phenomena and the fact that 99.9% of what we do is learned, including such basic behaviors as walking and talking. Once we learn something and do it over and over again, it becomes automatic. Then we forget we learned it and may erroneously conclude these learned responses are really "natural" responses, and therefore, not changeable.

Romantic Block #7. My partner should sacrifice his/her desires for mine.

This ultimate proof of love, *self-sacrifice*, is the central theme in this ideal. If you give up all things for your partner, that will assure your partner of love. The problem with self-sacrifice is that it depletes the giver's motivation to give. When this happens, love sought results in love denied.

Romantic Block #8. Sex with my partner must be great all the time.

Great sex is the barometer of love - no low pressure, please! If problems are encountered or if interest is low resulting in poor sexual performance, there can be no other explanation except that you are falling out of love with your partner, or you are falling in love with someone else.

Romantic Block #9. My partner should never forget anything or make mistakes when it comes to me.

This ideal requires you to place your partner's priorities at the top of the list. It doesn't matter if you have a different set of priorities, your partner's priorities should be considered first. Your partner should be the center of your universe. The demand for perfection from your partner requires that you devote yourself to the important events on your partner's calendar of events.

Romantic Block #10. Our love will solve all our problems.

This ideal eliminates the need for hard work and effort in managing your relationship.

153

APPENDIX B / What If Something Goes Wrong! Troubleshooting the Process - Part II
Communication Problems, Romantic Blocks and Low Motivation

Actually, nothing is needed but love. Love, the magic potion, makes the "bad" things go away, the difficult things easy, and the complex things simple.

Romantic Block #11. <u>We should not have any conflicts, differences, or quarrels.</u>

This idea is similar to Romantic Ideal #10. It presumes the two of you to be <u>so</u> in love that no conflicts or differences are possible. You as one-half, and your partner as the other half, unite to form the perfect whole.

The elimination of romantic "shoulds" will enable you to more realistically assess, challenge, and change yourself and your relationship and bring you satisfaction, joy and happiness. Adherence to romantic ideals like the ones above will foul the expectation process and bring disappointment and dissatisfaction.

LOW MOTIVATION

When someone lacks interest, or just doesn't care, there will be little effort expended in any direction. If you or your partner have low motivation, it will usually show up in a number of ways. This section of the guide should help you to identify low motivation and hopefully, do something about it. I say hopefully because you are not responsible for your partner's motivation, your partner is. You may be able to do something about your own level of motivation, but not your partner's. Getting your partner to read this section of the book may help, so shove it under your partner's nose and hope it is read.

"Feelings have to be there first!"

This idea requires emotional energy in order to get anything started. Strong feelings are necessary before any action is undertaken. To work at something without the requisite feeling is "wrong" and should be discouraged.

The idea is rooted in the notion that human feelings point to the truth. It also implies that working hard first to create a good emotional outcome is a waste of time and requires <u>too</u> much effort.

Exercise 30.

Take on a task that you have no motivation for doing or you feel neutral about. For example, read a non-interesting magazine or book. Force yourself to do it. When you do it, do it intensely, really get into it, but just for a short period of time, like 5 minutes or so. Go ahead and do it now!

What was it like? Did you get anything out of forcing yourself? How do you feel? If you answer any of the questions positively or negatively, you can now see how doing something "generates" emotion, and that emotions do not have to be there first in order to act. In fact, the positive or negative emotions you have created will now act as motivating forces in your life.

NOT TAKING IT SERIOUSLY ENOUGH

A reasonable effort occurring over a reasonable period of time is usually required to attain desired outcomes or changes. Obviously, it requires that serious attention be paid to the task at hand. In order to get the ball rolling, it may be necessary to clearly present your desires and preferences to your partner. Tell her/him how you feel! Tell him/her some of the major dissatisfactions that exist for you! Tell her/him some of the potential consequences that might occur if nothing is done! Ask him/her about areas of dissatisfaction that he/she might be experiencing!

STOPPING TOO SOON

Low motivation often results in stopping the process too soon. The consequences of this decision are clear. The opportunity to review all the expectations that are important to you and your partner will be lost. Make sure LFT isn't operating here ("This is too hard to continue any longer!"). Remember, you are the only one responsible for getting what you want out of life. And, you may have to push!

155

APPENDIX B / What If Something Goes Wrong! Troubleshooting the Process - Part II
Communication Problems, Romantic Blocks and Low Motivation

FAILURE TO MONITOR THE PROGRESS

Failing to monitor your progress on a continuing basis may result in you or your partner thinking, "What's the use, we're not getting anywhere", or "It doesn't feel like we're making enough progress to go any further". It is very important to assess your progress at each step along the way. When changes are made or new change strategies planned, reward yourself and each other for the effort put forth. Monitoring your progress gives you the opportunity to reward yourself and your partner. It's a kind of "payoff" that makes continuing the process "easier".

LACK OF SKILLS OR KNOWLEDGE

You or your partner may not automatically possess the communication skills or knowledge about relationship management. It may be necessary for some work to be done to fill the knowledge/skill void. Reading is probably the most readily available resource for most of us. Check the reading list in Appendix F, or contact your local library for help in locating materials on personal communication. If you are still experiencing problems after reading and practicing some of what you have read, you may want to consider taking a course or seminar offered at a community college or through an adult education program in your public school system.

NOTES

Appendix C

ADDITIONAL METHODS AND TECHNIQUES

The techniques described below have been shown to be helpful in controlling excessive emotional responses frequently experienced during the expectation-sharing process. Clients engaged in therapy are often helped with good success with these and other methods. If you wish to explore these techniques in more detail, consider some of the suggested reading materials in Appendix F.

Disputing Your Should Statements And Attributions

When you are emotionally disturbed and have determined what you are telling yourself to get so disturbed, simply ask,

WHY?

Ask **WHY** the things you are telling yourself are TRUE. Usually you will be able to see elements of *non-truth* in your thoughts when you do this. One of the best ways of training yourself to ask **WHY** is to write your statements, your questions, and your answers on paper.

> ### Example:
>
> **Statement** - Things must go my way!
>
> **Question** - *WHY* must things go my way?
>
> **Answer** - Things don't have to go my way, although it would be nice.

Basically, there are three *thinking* steps to follow, then a *doing* step.

1. You *Identify* what you are thinking.
2. You *Challenge* your thoughts.
3. You *Re-State* your original thinking.
4. You *Change Your Behavior* to go along with the New Thinking.

When your thinking is more precise, your emotions are likely to reflect the reality of the situation. You will be in a better position to respond (act) within that reality. Being careful not to attribute "false" characteristics to a situation or person will benefit you immensely in your dealings with any situation.

Example:

1. Original thoughts (Identification) - "He's always eating. Doesn't he know any better? After all, there is plenty of evidence that suggests overeating is bad for you. I can't stand people who overindulge! What a 'waste' he is!"

2. Question (Challenge) - "Why shouldn't he overeat even though it is bad for him? Why can't I stand him overeating? How is he a 'waste' for overeating?"

3. Answer (Re-statement) - "He can eat all he wants, he's in charge of his behavior. I can stand him overeating, I have for years. He does many other things that have a great deal of benefit for himself and others, so he isn't a total 'waste'."

4. Statements Leading to Behavior Change - "I wish he wouldn't eat so much. It certainly isn't good for him, so what I'll do, instead of yelling at him, is to educate him more by watching the health channel on cable TV when we're home together."

Rational Emotive Imagery

This is an imaginative technique, developed by Maultsby and adapted by Ellis for REBT, where you mentally visualize a situation that leads to some undesirable emotional upset. As you "see" the situation in your mind, you make yourself "feel" upset. You allow yourself to feel upset for a minute or so. While still "seeing" the situation in your imagination and are still feeling upset, you change your feelings and make yourself feel less disturbed. When you have gotten yourself less disturbed, stop the imagery, and determine how you got yourself less upset. Write down how your thinking changed as you were making yourself less disturbed. Plan on repeating the imagery technique over and over again until you free yourself of those disturbed feelings.

Example:

You get angry when you see your partner overeating, yell at him, and tell him he's going to kill himself. Mealtime, instead of being an enjoyable experience, has turned into a real "distasteful" time for the whole family. You want to change, but are finding it very difficult. Try the imagery technique.

Go to a quiet, private place. Close your eyes and begin to imagine yourself sitting at the table with your partner. Imagine you are watching him "gobble" down an enormous amount of food, despite your protestations. Let yourself begin to feel upset (anger, anxiety, etc., whatever feelings you might have in the situation). Continue to feel upset as you continue to watch him overeat. Now, even though he is continuing to overeat, make yourself feel less disturbed. Change the anger, anxiety, or whatever intense feelings you are experiencing to only regret, irritation, or concern. When you have done that, stop the imagery and on a piece of paper write the things you "told" yourself to get less disturbed. See if they are similar to the re-statements referred to in the disputing section above.

Keep practicing, using this technique, over and over again, until the disturbed feelings have been replaced with less disturbed feelings.

Humor and Exaggeration

These techniques are useful when you want to put life's events and your responses to them in realistic perspective. All too often we make things worse than they are, take them too seriously, and make ourselves unnecessarily unhappy. Looking for the humorous aspects of life's experiences is an important method of maintaining an emotional balance.

Example:

See your "overeating" partner as part of a side show in a carnival, or having difficulty getting through a door, or difficulty tying his shoes, and LAUGH about it. This will help you moderate your negative emotional and behavioral response to the situation. Keep in mind that the use of this method is not designed to have you condone the "overeating" but to deal with it more realistically.

Exaggerating negative views we have adopted can also be helpful in placing them in realistic perspective. Our views and our responses become more vivid to us when they are magnified and exaggerated. We become more aware of their inappropriateness and engage in a more determined effort to rid ourselves of them.

Example:

When you want something to go your way and you are feeling angry that it isn't, lay down on the floor and kick and scream about it, demanding that it go your way. Experience how inappropriate your "demandingness" is. Do this for other things that are disturbing you.

Relaxation Training and Exercise

Learning to relax can be an important method for getting your emotions under control, at least temporarily. Forcing yourself to focus on your body and the pleasurable sensations it can produce when relaxed is a distraction technique that will, when properly done, alter your emotional state. This is an important thing to do, especially when you are highly and negatively emotionally aroused. Relaxation requires focused concentration resulting in a temporary respite from your usual thinking activity. Vigorous exercise works just like relaxation and provides you with temporary relief from emotional distress. Use it when you are in an emotionally aroused state. When you're not thinking irrationally, your emotional disturbance will diminish. Unfortunately, your emotional disturbance will return when you resume your "old" thinking. Relaxation and exercise techniques do not alter your philosophy.

Many books have been written on the subject of relaxation and physical exercise and are available at your local bookstore, library or in Appendix F, our suggested Reading List. Pick up a few of these resources and try your hand at it.

NOTES

NOTES

Appendix D

NEGOTIATING PROCESS FORM
AND
LIST OF DESIRABLE TRAITS

NEGOTIATING PROCESS FORM

Name_____   Date_____

Time_____   Place_____

Privacy Insured? (Y) (N)

Expectation_____

_____

_____

Definitions_____

_____

_____

Importance Score_____ Performance Score_____

Checklist:

A. Have you clearly presented the above to your partner?

B. Have you received feedback from your partner?

C. Have you given your partner confirmation of the feedback?

D. Have clarifications been given regarding the meaning of the expectation?

Discussion Notes_____

_____

_____

_____

_____

_____

_____

_____

_____

Checklist:

A. Have you been compromising?

B. Have you been accepting?

C. Have you been keeping your emotions under control?

D. Have you included the what, where, how, whom, and
   when of the expectation?

E. Have you presented the "problematic nature" of the expectation?

Coming to Terms_____

_____
_____
_____
_____
_____
_____

Checklist:

A. Is the issue understood?
B. Has the work that is necessary to effect change been clearly presented?
C. Has the commitment to change been given?
D. Has the time frame been established?

Monitoring Notes_____

_____
_____
_____
_____
_____
_____
_____

Score Changes_____

©1988 David R. Lima

A GENERAL TRAIT/CHARACTERISTIC/BEHAVIOR LIST

The following list of behaviors and traits is from Tom Miller's book <u>Unfair Advantage</u>. The list may help you to formulate your personal list of expectations by stimulating your thinking.

adaptability	adaptable	admitting mistakes
adventurous	affectionate	aggressive
ambitious	amiable	analytic
anticipation	appearance	articulate
assertive	athletic	authentic
benevolent	bilingual	boy-friending
brave	broad-minded	brothering
calm	careful	caring
charismatic	charitable	charming
cheerful	chic	civil
clean	clear headed	communicative
compassion	compatible	competitive
complexion	composure	compromise
concentration	common sense	concern
concise	confident	confrontative
congenial	congruence	conscientious
considerate	consistent	conversational
conviction	convincing	cooperative
coordination	cordial	courageous
courteous	creative	curious
daughtering	daughter-in-lawing	decent
decisive	dedication	dependable
determination	diplomatic	disciplinarian
dynamic	efficient	endurance
energy level	entertaining	enthusiasm
extemporaneous	fair	far-sightedness
faithful	fashionable	fast thinker
fathering	father-in-lawing	feminine
flexible	follow-through	forceful

forgiving	frank	friendly
frugal	gentle	genuine
generous	girl-friending	good-humored
graceful	granddaughtering	grandfathering
grandmothering	grandsoning	grateful
handiness	hardiness	hard worker
healthiness	helpful	honest
hopeful	hospitable	humble
humorous	husbanding	inner-directed
innovative	intelligent	interested
interesting	jolly	joyful
kind	knowledgeable	loving
loyal	logical	manliness
masculine	mechanical	merciful
methodical	modest	monogamous
moral	mothering	mother-in-lawing
musical	neat	neighborly
nice	objectivity	observant
open minded	opportunistic	organized
patient	peaceful	perceptive
persistent	personality	perspective
persuasive	planning	playful
pleasant	polite	popular
practical	pragmatic	predictable
productive	proficient	prompt
proper	provider	prudence
punctual	purposeful	rational
realistic	reasonable	reassuring
receptive	reciprocal	reflective
reliability	religious	respectful
responsible	reverent	romantic
sense of humor	sensible	sexual
sexy	sincere	sistering
sister-in-lawing	skeptical	smart
sociable	soning	son-in-lawing

sophisticated	spunkiness	stable
steady	stimulating	story teller
straight forward	strong	studious
stylish	subtle	successful
supportive	sympathetic	systematic
tactful	talkative	tasteful
teaching	teamwork	tender
thankful	thorough	thoughtful
thrifty	tidy	tolerant
tranquil	traveled	troubleshooter
trustful	trusting	truthful
unbiased	understanding	unprejudiced
unselfish	upstanding	useful
utility	valiant	virile
virtuous	vocabulary	vocal
well groomed	well meaning	well read
well spoken	well thought of	wherewithal
witty	wifing	wishful
worldly wise	workability	workmanship
zestful	worship	youthful

NOTES

NOTES

Appendix E

ADDITIONAL SELECTED LISTS OF EXPECTATIONS

The following lists of expectations are provided to assist you in preparing your unique profile of traits, characteristics, and behaviors that you consider desirable in a partner. They represent lists created, defined and utilized by clients during their course of work with me. The lists have not been edited.

LIST NO. 1

A. Capable -   in an enterprising way. Works their way through a situation with a minimum of outside assistance.

B. Intelligent/Clever - quick on the uptake, ability to arrive at an intellectual intimacy in the relationship, on the "same wavelength" intellectually. Ability to get the other to see the other side without "forcing" one to see it. Be in control and have somewhat the "upper hand", but not all the time, of course.

C. Open-mindedness - staying open to discussion of the other's point of view without avoiding the discussion. Listening to other points of view first, talking later.

D. Awareness of Self - knows what to expect of himself, knows how he ticks, has a handle on himself. Takes time to be introspective, takes time to think it over before he responds.

E. Stable -   has a system of values and how he chooses to live his life is based on these standards. These values are known to me and can be relied upon not to change without warning (discussion).

F. Interest in the world - understanding and interest in history, world events,
    around him   politics. Open to such topics and their impact on us and others.

G. Sensitivity/ - Tenderness

emotionally tuned in to me, in depth. Ability to react and adapt to mood of partner. May stop activities to tune in; asks, probes.

H. Pride -

pride in self achievements, appearance, and surroundings. Takes the extra measure in each task started, pays attention to detail.

I. Consideration/ - Integrity/Consistency

conscientious behavior that shows respect for the other, shows that awareness of the other is present. Listens, does not go off in one direction without discussion, and after discussion follows through with joint decision. Shows sincerity by doing what was said would be done, follow- through, not weaseling out of things, playing games or being dishonest.

J. Zest for living -

emotional intensity in and when doing things, listening to music, going to movies, even the "little moments".

LIST NO. 2
(An example of a long list)

A. Neighborly, charismatic, friendly, personable, hospitable, interesting, charming, sociable, pleasant, cordial.
   One who enjoys others and who others like to be around.

B. Cheerful, good humored, joyful, jolly, humorous, witty, sense of humor.
   One who can laugh at himself and things and make you laugh.

C. Calm, peaceful, tranquil.
   When he is with you, you have a sense of peace and rest.

D. Stimulating.
   One who makes you think for yourself.

E. Trusting.
   Has faith in others.

F. Supportive, reassuring.
   Has faith in you and your decisions.

G. Interested.
   Listens as well as talks, not just hearing.

H. Perceptive, observant.
   Can tell when you are upset or hurting and responds.

I. Loving, caring, dependable, compassion, concern.
   Can be counted on to help you out when required.

J. Nice, decent.
   One who is morally and ethically oriented.

K. Humble, modest.
   One who is not filled with own self-importance.

L. Helpful, cooperative.
   Will help with things and will know when help is needed and when it is not.

M. Courteous, polite, considerate, thoughtful.
   Is pleasant to be around and does small unasked for surprises and gestures.

N. Affectionate.
   Likes to touch and have physical closeness.

O. Compatible.
   Enjoys the out-of-doors and activities that I enjoy.

P. Hard worker, inner directed, conscientious.
   Cares that he does a good job when doing something.

Q. Provider, generous, kind, unselfish, charitable.
   Is willing to share or take care of someone without thought of his own cost and time.

R. Strong, decisive, responsible, confident.
Has strength of his own convictions and stands by them.

S. Practical, common sense.
Is realistic in what he thinks, knows the difference between what is possible and what is not probable.

T. Trustful, reliable, consistent, follow-through.
Follows through on what he said he was going to do unless a reasonable reason for not doing so.

U. Grateful, thankful.
Appreciates when someone does things for him.

V. Prompt, punctual.
Is within reasonable time of what was set.

W. Forgiving, understanding.
Is tolerant of others' mistakes and non-condemning.

X. Broad-minded, admits mistakes, open-minded, reasonable, tolerant.
Admits he may be wrong or others have a right to a different opinion.

Y. Adaptability, flexible, composure.
Can make changes in plans and adjust with no hassle.

Z. Adaptable.
Can be satisfied with the situation although not exactly to his liking.

AA. Unprejudiced, respectful, diplomatic, fair.
Can accept people as they are without being judgemental.

BB. Communicative.
Will discuss different things, ideas, and expresses feelings easily.

CC. Authentic, genuine, congruent.
Accepts the way he is and doesn't try to show a different side to the public.

DD. Enthusiasm, anticipation.
Gets excited or gets a kick out of things.

EE. Curious, intelligence.
Wants to know more and thinks things over.

FF. Playful.
Enjoys horsing around.

LIST NO. 3

A. Don't dwell on the past.
Accept past mistakes, forgive self, and go on from there. Therefore, there will be less guilt and self-damning, and happiness will increase.

B. Be more tolerant.
Listen first, rather than evaluate immediately. Don't think that the answer must be found right away.

C. Be more empathetic.
Tune in with understanding to the feelings present rather than coming up with rational challenges first.

D. Be more affectionate.
Give more hugs, kisses, initiate the physical touching.

E. Be more flexible/spontaneous/adventurous.
When "out-of-the-blue" ideas come up, don't avoid them, instead go with them. Don't plan as much.

F. Allow for more traditional family elements.
Cooking more, eating together as a family, going to activities together, vacations.

G. Appreciate the fine arts more.

Go to museums, join cultural groups, collect fine arts.

H. Develop an appreciation for sports.

Get involved in baseball, football, basketball, etc. Go to games or watch it on TV.

LIST NO. 4

Bill had the following expectations of Jane.

A. Be contemporary and up to date.

Read more, be able to discuss items in the news.

B. Be more adaptable.

If plans are not able to be carried out, don't get so emotionally upset, that other plans can't be arranged.

C. Be more independent.

Learn to do more things alone. Go shopping, to the movies, or out with friends without always requiring the other's presence.

D. Be more initiating in the sexual area.

Start it more, be more seductive, try some sexual behaviors not yet tried.

E. Don't read meanings into his actions.

Instead of going on assumptions, ask.

Jane had the following expectations of Bill.

A. Spend more time together.

Arrange to do things together, rather than with separate (outside) group of friends.

B. Communicate more.

Sit down and talk about problems that come up, instead of leaving the problem to be worked out with one or the other.

C. Develop areas of commonality.

> *Do more things together, especially games and sports.*

D. Show more non-sexual affection.

> *Give hugs and kisses for no reason at all. Do it without touching the breasts.*

E. Be more initiating in the sexual area.

> *Act like sex is wanted, show horniness.*

F. Compromise more.

> *Be willing not to always have it go your way.*

G. Share more of the household tasks.

> *Clean up inside the house and help with other chores, instead of just washing the car.*

LIST NO. 5

"His" expectations of "Her"

A. Don't emotionally overreact to events.

> *Keep panic response from showing, especially in front of the kids.*

B. Don't associate so much with neighbors who have an "ain't it awful" attitude.

> *Find new friends and neighbors, instead of limiting it to just the one.*

C. Don't "put down" efforts at doing household chores.

> *Relax, don't be so perfectionistic, demanding and critical of the job he does.*

D. Give him more space.

> *Give 15 minutes of rest and relaxation after he comes home from work, let him go fishing alone, and go along with it uncomplainingly when he asks for privacy.*

E. Lose weight.
   Lose 35 pounds in the next year.

"Her" expectations of "Him"

A. Take more safety precautions with the children.
   Keep them from the street, use seat belts when in the car, don't let them ride their bikes alone.

B. Be more accessible for discussions.
   When she asks to talk, agree, sit down and force himself to stay and discuss, not avoid.

C. Reduce perfectionistic thinking.
   Be more adaptable, let things become part of his life as they come up, rather than running from them when they do. Be willing to change plans.

D. Be faithful.
   Don't have any extra-marital affairs.

LIST NO. 6

A. Wants him to show emotions openly and honestly.
   Sadness, sympathy, cries when hurt, is moved and can show it when affected by something tender or sentimental, shows unreserved joy. Doesn't mope around, doesn't get irritated unexplainably, doesn't get physically violent, instead talks about anger and irritability.

B. Wants him to be open and communicate honestly.
   Talk, talk, talk. Listens, gives non-verbal communication (eye contact, a touch), understands even though he may not agree. When I am upset, asks about it, questions. Doesn't clam up, realizes things just don't go away, doesn't put down my problems or ideas (silly, stupid).

C. Wants him to be my friend.

Realize that I'm a person first, and a wife second. Enjoy each other's company. Be able to be silly with each other without feeling embarrassed. Feel all the sharing, caring, liking, laughing, things that friends feel when with each other. Don't ignore my feelings and treat me like property. Respect the fact that we are together voluntarily, we do not have the sole rights to each other. Like me enough to try new things, even if they are not comfortable for you.

D. Someone I can share my religion with.

Shares the same basic belief, will share his beliefs with me. Doesn't mock my beliefs, can accept sharing my life with my religion.

E. Someone who is not overly jealous or possessive.

Doesn't make accusation without facts, doesn't watch my every move, doesn't restrict me from seeing people I want to see, doesn't make threatening remarks when jealous, doesn't always require an explanation.

F. Someone who is not preoccupied with sex.

See it more as an act of love, rather than an act of lust. Takes time with it, puts some romance in it from time to time. Respect my body, love it, not abuse it or use it. Be more caressing, looking, admiring before and after sex. Be more understanding when I don't initiate it, it doesn't mean I don't love you.

G. Wants him to be more humble.

Know and accept you have faults and short-comings, quit living life as some major competition. Accept that others have some traits that are "better" than yours. Give up the idea and action that you have to prove yourself. Be able to compliment an achievement greater than yours made by someone else. Don't stand in my way when I want to achieve something. Realize that I don't make you look foolish if I don't like a trait or behavior.

NOTES

Appendix F

SUGGESTED READING LIST

The following selected reading materials may prove helpful in understanding and exploring further many of the ideas presented in this book. These books may be purchased from Lima Associates, 8353 Mentor Ave., Mentor, OH 44060. Write for a catalog of publications, or call at 1-800-810-9011 or visit their web site at http://www.lima-associates.com.

BOOKS AND TAPES ON RATIONAL EMOTIVE BEHAVIOR THERAPY

A Guide To Rational Living by Albert Ellis. The most comprehensive work on rational psychotherapy for the lay-person.

A Primer of RET by Raymond DiGiuseppe. A concise, practical guide to RET.

The Silly Mind: Learning to Take Life Less Seriously by David Lima and Donald Scobel. Shows you a new way of evaluating your beliefs and changing them.

Three Minute Therapy by Michael Edelstein. Contains brief exercises designed to help you change your emotions.

How to Keep People from Pushing Your Buttons by Albert Ellis. Provides specific ways to keep people and events from getting you emotionally upset.

How to Stubbornly Refuse to Make Yourself Miserable About Anything, Yes Anything! by Albert Ellis. The message in this book is most emotional misery are unnecessary over-reactions and can be significantly reduced.

How to Control Your Anger Before It Controls You by Albert Ellis. Dr. Ellis explains how to control your anger when commonplace frustrations occur.

Anger: How to Live With It and Without It by Albert Ellis. Presents a step-by-step technique designed to help you explore and understand the roots and nature of your anger.

What Do I Do with My Anger: Hold It In or Let It Out? (audio tape) by Raymond DiGiuseppe. Learn how to avoid giving in to anger.

BOOKS ON MARRIAGE

A Guide to Successful Marriage by Albert Ellis. Devoted to love and sex aspects of marriage.

Intimate Connections by David Burns. Advice, case histories and exercises designed to help you form intimate relationships.

The Art of Living Single by Michael Broder. A positive approach to living on your own.

The Art of Staying Together: A Couple's Guide to Intimacy and Respect by Michael Broder. Explores the many choices available to couples on how to conduct a relationship.

Marriage Is A Loving Business by Paul Hauck. Describes proven methods for getting more love out of your marriage.

OTHER BOOKS AND TAPES TO HELP YOU OVERCOME EMOTIONAL DISTURBANCE

Feeling Good: The New Mood Therapy by David Burns. Best-selling book designed to help you overcome depression.

Feeling Good Handbook by David Burns. Powerful techniques described to overcome a full range of everyday emotional problems.

Meditations for Overcoming Depression (audio tape) by Joan Borysenko. Stress and anxiety-reducing meditations designed to alleviate the symptoms associated with depression.

Feeling Good (audio tape) by David Burns. Describes self-defeating thought patterns and explains how to replace them.

The Perfectionist's Script for Self-Defeat (audio tape) by David Burns. Helps identify perfectionistic tendencies and how they work against you.

Calm Beneath the Waves: A Tape for Panic, Anxiety, Desperation and Hopelessness (audio tape) by Bill O'Hanlon. Describes ideas to give you immediate relief from emotional upset.

RELAXATION AND MEDITATION TAPES

Imageries (audio tape) by Claudia Black. Provides a variety of ways in which to experience your inner self.

Meditations for Forgiveness (audio tape) by Joan Borysenko. Describes transforming pain into peace and forgiveness.

Meditations for Relaxation and Stress Reduction (audio tape) by Joan Borysenko. Breath centered and stretching exercises designed to help you restore body, mind and spirit.

Relaxation Exercise (audio tape) by Michael Broder. Provides a daily regimen of relaxation exercises and music.

Invitation to Relax (audio tape) by Michael Mahoney. A gentle exercise for deepening your natural ability to relax.

Mirror Time (audio tape) by Michael Mahoney. An exercise in self-care.

NOTES

Appendix G

SOURCES OF PROFESSIONAL HELP

This book may be helpful, as many self-help books are, in achieving happiness and enjoying your life more fully. However, there may be no substitute for face-to-face personal counseling or therapy. This is especially true if a serious problem is identified in the course of reading this book and "working" the program. If you encounter difficulty in completing the tasks described in this book, that may be reason enough for you to seek professional assistance. I have identified a number of sources you may wish to contact.

NATIONAL AND INTERNATIONAL

Albert Ellis Institute for Rational Emotive Behavior Therapy, 45 E. 65th St., New York, N.Y. 10021. Ph.: (212) 535-0822. Web Site: <www.rebt.org> The Institute maintains a nationwide list of qualified professionals who have met certain standards and can provide you with the counseling/therapy you desire.

National Association of Social Workers, Inc., 750 First Street, N.E., Suite 700, Washington, D.C. 20002. Ph.: (202) 408-8600. NASW maintains a national and international register of clinical social workers that contains the names of over 8,000 qualified clinical social workers. Contact NASW for further information.

American Psychological Association, 750 First St., NE, Washington, D.C. 20002-4242 Ph.: (202)336-5500. Web Site: <www.helping.apa.org/refer> APA maintains a list of state psychology associations who can refer you to qualified professionals who can provide services for emotional and relationship problems.

American Association of Marriage and Family Therapy, 1133 15th Street, NW. Ste. 300, Washington, D.C. 20005-2710 (202) 452-0109. Web Site: <www.aamft.org> This office can be contacted for the location of and referral to a qualified professional anywhere in the United States.

Lima Associates, 8353 Mentor Ave., Mentor, Ohio 44060. Ph: (440)255-3299. Web Site: <www.lima-associates.com> This group maintains a national list of qualified professionals in rational emotive behavior therapy and would be happy to provide a referral.

LOCAL

Contact your **"Community Information Service"**. Look under the heading "Social Service Organizations" in the Yellow Pages of your telephone book. A community information service can provide you with a referral after you tell them what you want.

Contact your local **"Mental Health Center"** or **"Mental Health Board"**. These two agencies will be able to provide you with information and/or the counseling services desired.

Contact your **health insurance plan**. Most plans have a "mental health" component and can refer you to a professional who is part of their provider network.

Contact your **local welfare department** usually listed in the phone book under "County Offices". Your local office of the United Way may also be able to provide assistance to you. In larger population areas there may be a Jewish Family Service office or a Catholic Social Service office. They will be able to direct you to the right resource.

Additional listings in the Yellow Pages may prove helpful. Check under **"Clinics"**, **"Social Workers"**, **"Marriage and Family Counselors"**, or **"Psychologists"**. When you go about selecting someone this way, make sure you ask for their qualifications and their areas of expertise.

REFERENCES

Burns, D.D. _Feeling Good._ New York: Morrow, 1980.

Ellis, A. _The Nature of Disturbed Marital Relationships._ New York: Institute for Rational Living, 1964.

Ellis, A. _Unhealthy Love: Its Causes and Treatment._ New York: Institute for Rational Living, 1973.

Ellis, A., & Becker, I. _A Guide to Personal Happiness._ N. Hollywood: Wilshire Books, 1982.

Ellis, A., and Harper, R. _A New Guide to Rational Living._ N. Hollywood: Wilshire Books, 1975.

Epictetus. _The Works of Epictetus._ Boston: Little, Brown, 1899.

Gibran, K. _The Prophet._ New York: Knopf, 1923.

Hauck, P.A. _Marriage is a Loving Business._ Philadelphia: Westminister, 1972.

Miller, T. _Unfair Advantage._ Skaneateles, N.Y.: Lakeside, 1983. (formerly titled _So You Secretly Suspect You're Worthless…_)

NOTES

INDEX

ABC's of Emotions, 45

Absolute imperative, 20

Anger, 43, 126-128

Anxiety, 132-138

Anxiety, Discomfort, 133-134

Anxiety and love, 20-21

Appreciation and Resentment Sessions, 59-63

Attribution/Assumption error, 149

Awfulizing, 35, 128-129

Challenging the B, 45

Change, 54

Cognitive Distortions, 142-144

Cognitive Mutations, 21-22

Communication, 55

Communication errors, 57

Communication method, 58-59

Communication problems, 147-149

Condemnation, 35, 131-132

Controlling Excessive Negative Emotions, 45-49

Defensiveness, 137-138

Demandingness, 35

Depression, 140-142

Desperate love, 20

Dichotomous thinking, 143

Differences, 53

Disputing, 157-158

Disqualifying the positive, 144

Emotional Interferences, 125-142

Emotional reasoning, 19, 142

Emotional stability, 41

Expectations, Defining (Exercise), 76-77

Expectations, Identifying (Exercise), 68-69

Expectations, Importance of, 81-83

Expectations, listing, 71-76, 171-179

Faulty conclusions, 21

Fear of failure, 136-137

Feedback error, 148

Guilt, 44, 138-140

Humor and Exaggeration, 159-160

Identifying the B (Exercise), 47-49

Importance Rating Scale, 82

Infants Failure to Thrive, 23

Intolerance, 130-131

Irrational Expectations, 35-36

Jumping to conclusions, 142

Kahlil Gibran on Marriage, 53-54

Labeling/Mislabeling, 144

Love, defined, XIII, 26

Love, feelings, XIII

Love, healthy, 26-27

Love masks, social, biologic, romantic, 24-26

Love needs, 23-24

Love, selfish, 26

Low frustration tolerance (LFT), XIV, 44, 121-125

Magnification/minimization, 144

Mental filter, 143

Mental jump-shift, 22

Minimum Acceptable Level of Partner's

   Performance Scale (MALP), 84

Minimal interaction error, 148-149

Motivation, Low, 153-154

Needful thinking, 20-22

Negotiating, 54-55, 91-107

Negotiating Case excerpt, 98-106

Negotiating, ground rules, 94-95

Negotiating Process Form, 164-165

Negotiating, steps, 95-98

Neurotic love, 20-21

Neurotic reasons for marrying, 23-24

Non-verbal meaning (Exercise), 56-57

Overgeneralization, 143-144

Personalization, 143

Practical and Impractical Expectations, 36

Professional Help, 185-186

Pursuit of happiness, 27

Rational-Emotive Imagery (REI), 158-159

Rational-Emotive Behavior Therapy (REBT), XI

Rational expectations, 34

Reading list, 181-183

Reasons for a Relationship (Exercise), 26

Relationship management, XIV

Relaxation training, 160

Review and Subsequent Sessions, 111-118

Romantic blocks, 150-153

Self-Righteousness, 44

Shame, 138-140

Should statements, 143

Sources of help, 185-186

Symptom Stress, 135-136

Trait list, 166-168

Trouble Shooting, Part I, 121-144

Trouble Shooting, Part II, 147-155

ABOUT THE AUTHOR

After nearly ten years of active practice, Mr. Lima became keenly aware of the ineffectiveness of most counseling approaches, especially those that stressed support or environmental manipulation. He became acquainted with <u>REBT</u> (Rational Emotive Behavior Therapy), an approach that focuses on the role of thinking (beliefs) in emotional disturbances. Subsequently, he enrolled in the training program at the Albert Ellis Institute for Rational Emotive Behavior Therapy, New York, and is now an Associate Fellow of the Institute. He uses REBT in his work with individuals, couples, families, and groups.

David Lima has been practicing clinical social work since 1966. He received his Master of Social Work degree from Florida State University in that year and began his career as a psychiatric social worker. In 1971 he was appointed the executive director of an outpatient mental health facility for adolescents and young adults. During this time he served as marriage counselor for the county Domestic Relations court and served as a consultant to a variety of social service agencies. In addition to his clinical private practice, Mr. Lima currently sponsors continuing education workshops for behavioral healthcare professionals. Lima Associates is approved as a provider of Continuing Professional Education throughout the United States by national professional organizations and state licensing and credentialing authorities.

Mr. Lima is a member of the National Association of Social Workers, the Academy of Certified Social Workers and the Academy of Family Mediators. He is a Registered Clinical Social Worker (NASW) and a Licensed Independent Social Worker (State of Ohio).

Mr. Lima lives with his wife, Nancy in Mentor, Ohio.

To arrange a speaking engagement by David Lima, please contact:
Lima Associates, 8353 Mentor Avenue, Mentor, Ohio 44060, (800) 810-9011.